T0171489

The Greatest
COMMANDMENT

Matthew 22:37

David T. Steineker

WestBow
PRESS
A DIVISION OF THOMAS NELSON

Author Credits: 2006-2007 Who's Who in Professionals and Executives for www.KentuckyFamily.com

WestBow Press books may be ordered through booksellers or by contacting:

WestBow Press
A Division of Thomas Nelson
1663 Liberty Drive
Bloomington, IN 47403
www.westbowpress.com
1-(866) 928-1240

ISBN: 978-1-4497-0666-1 (sc)
ISBN: 978-1-4497-0877-1 (hc)
ISBN: 978-1-4497-0669-2 (e)

Library of Congress Control Number: 2010940629

Print information available on the last page.

WestBow Press rev. date: 7/2/2014

Contents

Preface

The book is titled "The Greatest Commandment", since following it is a choice and the choices you make will determine your fate. Many have read or have heard the greatest commandment but chose not to follow it. Behaving like the Good Samaritan requires work, since very often we do not associate with our neighbors. The Samaritan woman said to Jesus, "You are a Jew and I am a Samaritan woman. How can you ask me for a drink? (For Jews do not associate with Samaritans). (John 4:9) Love is an action word, thus understanding the importance of the greatest commandment and how it affects our destiny is the purpose of the book. When we say the pledge of allegiance the concept of our country being indivisible is a reference to our God being undividable. God created us on this Earth for the purpose of producing the child of God an eternal spirit; the greatest commandment defines how this is possible.

Sin is associated with not following the greatest commandment, since all of the law is built on it; the wages of sin is death. Death is an ending, so can God be understood? If God can't be understood, then sin makes no sense. If God can't be understood, then it's not my fault that I sin. God being defined without comprehension leads to justification for sinful behavior. For example, God said it was wrong to steal, lie, murder, but the scholar choses to promote God as incomprehensible; therefore the scholar can justify their sinful behavior as not their fault and that everybody will eventually go to heaven. The scholar seeks the praise of both men and women. When God is described as uncomprehend able Jesus is being left out of the picture resulting in the meaning of life being misunderstood. An eternal utopia of sameness would be a description of Jesus being left out of the picture, because a universe filled with only dark matter and nothing would be boring and expected. Heaven and earth will disappear, but my words will never disappear (Matthew 24:35). If the reader thinks he or she can predict all the things that God can do, then expect some big surprises. A virgin birth of Jesus is an evolutionary birth associated with an increase in chromosome number, thus human evolution from a lower species would require Adam and Eve to have experienced the same origin. The son is the image of the invisible God. (Colossians 1:15-17) Human evolution and the genesis story of creation are opposites. These opposites do not cancel each other out, they determine the possibilities. Luke 24:31 states then their eyes were opened and they recognized him, and he disappeared from their sight.

If you Love the Lord your God with all your Heart, Mind, Soul, then why is there a second law? The second law really displays the same principles as the first. This is why the first commandment is the greatest or most clear description of what God calls us to do. God is a Creator, and the law is a representation of how he builds. Love thy neighbor as thy self. God created both your neighbor and thy self; if you choose not to love your neighbor then you do not love God with all your Mind, Heart, and Soul. (Philippians 2:3) As a descendant of original sin, we lack the authority to judge ourselves better than others; only Jesus has the authority to instruct us about the commands of God because his intentions purely teach that your best is never good enough as illustrated with the seven woes spoken to the Jewish leaders. Why is you best never good enough? Your best creates selfish ambition to control the team instead of working to make the weak link stronger. John the Baptist did not have the authority to speak to King Herod like Jesus did to the Jewish leaders, since John's death reflects a descent from original sin. (Romans 6:23) How do you Love the Lord your God with all your Soul, Heart, and Mind? The second law is designed to be a general education law, master it and the first law will become clearer. The greatest commandment is a call to love as exemplified in the parable of the Good Samaritan.

Organization

This book is organized around the importance of Matthew 22:37, because Jesus states in Luke 10:27-28 what is required for eternal life. Eternal life requires absolute truth. What is absolute truth? An absolute truth is truth that will not turn into a lie over a long period of time. If God can't be understood, then sin makes no sense. The goal of the devil is to promote an incomprehensible God. If God is incomprehensible at his core, then miracles would be impossible since they represent an opposite of what is expected. Good and evil are not the same just like something (1 particle) and nothing (0) are not the same.

An example of absolute truth would be that love and hate are opposites and over a long period of time they will never be the same. I may not understand everything about God, but at his core he must be comprehensible otherwise Jesus would not have risen from the dead. The amount of understanding concerning the nature of God depends on your level of friendship with Jesus. If we are called to Love God, then what is God? The Son is the image of the invisible God. (Colossians 1:15-17) What does that mean? It means that God is with us. God is with us means that God is the something that moves through nothing to form all that you observe; even this book. The Son is the image of the invisible God, and the human spirit was created upon conception to be eternal. That is the reason for life on Earth. God created us on this Earth for the primary purpose of producing the eternal spirit.

In order to be a leader in any subject, the leader must be the best at the work or they are just a follower. This is the point of Jesus; he is the source of truth, since the word became flesh. He is the leader of truth, thus he is the way to understand God. God can be understood and Jesus makes that clear in Luke 10:27-28. Jesus answers the question as to what is the meaning of life. He is the life. What does that mean? Why are you living on Earth? What is the purpose of life? Is the flesh more important than the spirit? Not knowing what occurs after death makes us think that the flesh is more important and leaves us with no answer to what is the meaning of life. Solomon concluded that we should love God and follow his commands; however Solomon does not mention grace. Solomon reasons that God should be honored even if life is meaningless, since only God is eternal. Solomon put his trust in God even though he was not convinced that his spirit could be eternal, since he never mentions grace.

The New Testament defines the meaning of life and the Old Testament based on "an eye for an eye" shows how difficult life is without the gift of the Holy Spirit (John 20:23). When the body dies, then doubts arise about the strength of the spirit. If the spirit is not eternal, then life has no meaning for the individual. If it has no meaning for the individual, then Jesus would not have been inspired to leave heaven and come to Earth and suffer death on a cross to save the lost. The author is not the source of truth on the general education topics presented in this book, since the truth on these topics existed before his creation and he is only making light of them to the reader because of John the Baptist. Why John the Baptist? He did not have a large amount of land nor a big home with many servants. He did not publish any books of poetry nor did he write Revelation.

Why John the Baptist? He prepared the way! More model his behavior than any other person that has ever lived. John the Baptist exemplified the Good Samaritan. Is the reader preparing the way for the harvest that has yet to come? As Christians we are called to prepare the way for the return of Jesus. If the way is not prepared, then grace does not occur. I can't become Jesus, since I am pointing my finger at him when I am accused of sin. Scripture verses quoted in the book are from the KJV, so the reader may desire to use a NIV as a reference. This is a general education book, so each chapter will address issues that are unique to the topic. The plot of this text is driven by absolute truth. The subplot is driven by free will. The goal of the author is to provide the reader with the absolute truth on each topic, so that the reader can make their own decision about the topic based on free will. The decision the reader makes on each general education topic could be life changing, because the author encourages the reader share absolute truth with others. The author makes no claim to the absolute truth, nor will he deny it. Absolute truth will never change into a lie in an infinite universe; this is a reason the Bible is not written in chronological order.

Acknowledgements

I encourage the reader to believe in their dreams. I have had vivid dreams and in times of despair those dreams encouraged me not to give up or quit. I thank my parents for helping provide for my Education. A church is not a building; it is a body of believers, so I thank the church for supporting my growth as a Christian. This book was far from being easy to write, much research has been done and thoughtful defense of the general education topics presented has occurred both on the internet and in person. I thank my wife for helping me understand how difficult this book was to write. This book started soon after we married with a gradual accumulation of the general education topics over ten years. Without a doubt, I thank my wife for helping me take risks; otherwise I would still be in the boat with Peter afraid and of little faith and full of doubt. (Matthew 14: 29-31) Lastly, I thank my children Madelyn, Mason, Micah, and Melody for teaching me how to pray (Philippians 2:3). The goal of the Church is to promote child to adult love of God. When Jesus was an Adult the Devil led him up to a high place and showed him in an instant all the kingdoms of the world. And he said to him, I will give you all their authority and splendor, for it has been given to me, and I can give it to anyone I want to. So if you worship me, it will be all yours. (Luke 4:3-7) Wealth is too often associated with being a blessing from God, just examine King Solomon. Matthew 22:23 is not a commandment to be good it is a commandment to love all that is good, thus a percentage of author royalties from this book will go to support women that chose not to have an abortion. The author acknowledges God to be fully comprehendible as stated in 1 Corinthians 14:33; acknowledges himself as a sinner and thanks Jesus Christ for accepting the punishment as stated in Luke 20:36.

Chapter 1

Introduction

> No, this trick won't work . . . How on earth are you
> ever going to explain in terms of chemistry and
> physics so important a biological phenomenon as
> first love?
>
> **—Albert Einstein**

If you commit a crime and are found guilty, the fine or sentence associated with the verdict is a sacrifice meant to prevent you from repeating the crime. Which means the more you grow in Christ, the more you should miss him in the flesh. Thomas was a disciple of Christ, and he did not believe that Christ rose from the grave after being crucified until he looked upon Jesus with his own eyes and touched his nail pierced hands. Why does this matter? Thomas listened to the words of Jesus on many occasions and he believed the miracles Christ performed. Why does this matter? The purpose of the Christian is to prepare the way for the second coming of Christ. If the way is not prepared, then Christ will be rejected and God will be viewed as incomprehensible. Thomas rejected the resurrection until he witnessed it in the flesh. Jesus is not the God dictator who seeks to control us or make us work for him; this is the reason he did not tell Peter and John the Baptist how to live. Loving God is a choice that requires work. Preparing the way is like tilling the field, since a crop can't be planted in a field that has not been tilled. If people never experience kindness, self-control, gentles, the fruits of the spirit, then love of God is

1

meaningless to them. If you felt no love from the church, would you go forward and accept the free gift of salvation that Jesus offers all the end of each service and continue to be a member? Prepare the way, then you will see God; that is the reward.

Jesus could be living in your house right now based on what we are learning about the telomere and how the cell ages; telomerase prevents telomere shortening and replicative senescence. (http://mcb.berkeley.edu/ courses/ mcb135k/telomeres.html) Living things on the planet don't all have the same life span. Free will dictates that there must be a heaven and a hell. The question is, are you good enough to defeat Satan? To be victorious against Satan requires living a life free of evil decisions based upon loving all that is good. Just one lie is all it takes to resemble Satan and for him to say, "You are just like me, since you do not love God". For this reason many fear Satan, since resembling him makes us a child of his. Thus we have given him the power to mistreat us. This answers the question as to why bad things can happen to good people. Your attitude after the event reflects whom you serve.

Loving all that is good strengthens the chain of command. There is no "me" in the word team, since "me" has no love for the team Authority flows from the top down, thus trying to follow all of the commands like the rich young ruler in Luke 18:18-23 did from the bottom up showed he worked for his own glorification modeling the behavior of the devil. Jesus denied this type of leadership, since God knows what he is doing. God created the human being without any help from the human being. The rich young ruler tried to get into heaven his own way, since Heaven is not a place everyone will see and it is described as being better than Earth it was the objective of the rich young ruler to establish his importance. The devil is the opposite of Jesus Christ and Satan uses the law in the opposite direction to establish his kingdom in this world. The second commandment that Jesus Christ gave us is not a part of the Ten Commandments given by Moses to the Jewish people. This was the rich young ruler's conflict, he could not love his neighbor as himself. Often we just move away from the neighbors we do not like, or make rules that prevent them from joining the church or make it uncomfortable by constantly reminding them of their sin. When the rich young ruler ran up to Jesus and fell on his knees he was definitely out of his comfort zone. It is not easy to love people that clearly and visibly do not follow the law. This is the reason loving God requires work and those that boast of this work will not receive the grace offered to us from Jesus Christ.

Satan hates free will; he desires to tell you exactly what to do and if it were up to him only Hell would exist. Satan is by definition a control freak. (Mark 5:2-5) Legion was possessed by evil, so his behavior shows us the nature of evil. However Satan should not be feared, because Satan cannot fundamentally destroy or tear apart your spirit which means that spirit would no longer exist in Heaven or Hell. Why not to hell? That might be a decision of Moses. (John 5:45) A power of God concerns being remembered. (Matthew 26:24) (Matthew 18:6) This is the reason even the demons believe that God is real and obey his commands. (Luke 10:17) God has the power to create and destroy. (Revelation 21:8) According to Christian millennial theory there are four possibilities associated with the second coming of Jesus Christ. They are as follows: Post-tribulational Premillennialism, Pre-tribulational (dispensational) Premillennialism, Postmillennialism, and Amillennialism. All four have one thing in common. Jesus is coming again, and those who do not love God will experience the second death based on their own choice. The destruction of a spirit in the second death leaves no evidence of the spirit ever existing. This is the power of God, since it addresses accountability associated with an event that left someone thinking how could God let this happen? Your spirit does not know how to maintain its eternal state, no different than your mind does not know how to make your body live longer than 120 years, thus independence from God results in the decomposition of the spirit or second death.

Humbleness concerns recognizing that you can't accomplish the task alone and that you should ask for help, thus I encourage you to accept Christ and become a new creation. The task concerns defeating Satan, and he wants to destroy your freedom to make a choice. If it were up to Satan, only Hell would exist. Jesus has proven that he is capable of getting the job done. So, deny yourself like Christ did (Luke 22:42) and celebrate the Victory with him. (Matthew 4:1-9) It's all about the numbers. The numbers are far greater in heaven, because of Christ than in hell do to Satan. (John 5:25)

"For whosoever shall do the will of my Father which is in heaven, the same is my brother, and sister, and mother." (Matthew 12:50) This is the most significant statement given by Jesus to describe Heaven. This statement describes your Heavenly Significance! The will of the father concerns accepting the Son of God and becoming a new creation. It is a known fact that God is real, proven with countless miracles and endless mathematical evidence. The belief in God concerns his description. Either God is "Nothing" that created everything out of emptiness or God is

"Something" that can neither be created nor destroyed that is dependent on nothing. How God is recognized does matter, since truth can't be deceived!

How do miracles support the truth? A miracle is a record that an unprovable opposite has occurred. Miracles could be considered evidence other than math (zero doesn't equal one) that opposites are a part of the Universe and that our Universe is Infinite. An infinite universe lacks a beginning, so within it there is no one set past or a given future; it lacks a timeline. The son is the image of the invisible God. (Colossians 1:15-17) This scripture states God is present with us and not off somewhere in the distance as the all mighty uncomprehend able blend of something and nothing. Since it would have to be uncomprehend able blend of something and nothing to produce both something and nothing as stated in the Big Bang Theory—nothing appeared out of emptiness and nothing formed something. This is not new science it's Old Sadducees theology about the nature of God. In the Big Bang Theory if something eventually turns into nothing, then what is the purpose of the resurrection of the dead? The Sadducees included mainly priests and aristocratic families, whom had the authority to promote their disbelief in the resurrection of the dead to the Jewish people. Aristocrats believe in a class system, which promotes the "me" as being more important than the team. An Aristocrat is a ladder climber that promotes their own work, which is the reason for their doubt in the resurrection of the dead.

If the reader believes absolute truth and lies are interchangeable, then those that listen to the reader are being used for the purpose of financial gain. Fool me once shame on you; fool me twice and shame on me. Truth and lies are never interchangeable and will always be opposites as stated in Isaiah 40:8, 1 Peter1:25, and Matthew 24:35. Comparing Matthew 24:35 to John 3:16 reveals that our spirit is the only thing in the Universe that is truly similar in structure to our God and his word. If our spirit is not eternal, then 10^{150} years in heaven would seem like a blink of the eye compared to eternity. Time is relative to what one gets accustom to in the surroundings. Matthew 24:35 makes no mention of hell passing away, thus accountability is still being addressed in Matthew 10:28. God created your spirit using a specific ratio of himself. If that ratio is ever changed then you no longer exist as stated in Matthew 10:28, just like a change in your DNA would change your physical appearance. The devil is the author of destruction and seeks to destroy your spirit, because he does not love God. Suicide is a forgivable sin. Suicide is a tool the Devil uses to get the spirit to destroy itself in Hell by constantly reminding that spirit of its lack of worth. Often behaviors are repeated in life and it should not be surprising for the Devil to be literally described as a destroyer. Destroying you is a way he can show that God would have been better off had he not created you. Remember Satan was happy with creation until God created Adam and Eve. Genesis 1:31 tells us everything was very good at the end of the creation week, so Satan had not fallen yet. If God can't be understood, then sin makes no sense. The goal of the Devil is to promote an incomprehensible God. If Jesus Christ is incomprehensible, then the Devil has made his goal.

There was no period of time before the original creation. There was actually no time. God made time as well as matter and space http://www.creationtoday. org/when-did-satan-fall-from-heaven/. The author disagrees with the above statement, since it is based on theology before Jesus Christ came and was rejected by the Jewish leaders as the son of God or the one whom reveals the nature of God. God creates time since he is an eternal being. His movement is timeless, this is an amazing description of God and comprehensible otherwise nothing in the universe would be comprehensible. If there was no time before creation, then the definition of something eternal is false. Time is a mathematical measurement defined as Time = Distance / Velocity. When something moves over a specific distance at a certain velocity time is calculated. It takes 24 hours representing a count for the Earth to complete one rotation or spin and approximately 365 days to go all the way around the sun. If there was no time or matter before creation, then there would be no eternal Word as stated in Isaiah 40:8. Nothing lacks power to hold onto the Word, since it is empty or void of substance. Describing God as incomprehensible is not honorable to God and results from anger towards God because the wages of sin is death as Romans 6:23 states.

If emptiness nor nothing can make or hold onto the word, then truth and lies are the same. Since nothing would not have the ability to discern the difference between the two opposites.

Something that is eternal lacks a beginning and does not have an end.

According to the Big Bang opposites do not exist, because nothing created something and something will eventually turn back into nothing. Things that are finite have a birth and a death. Thus according to the Big Bang a truth will eventually turn into a lie, because it states that emptiness, nothing, and something are all interchangeable. A theory for everything is only possible if opposites do not exist.

David T. Steineker

If God is described as incomprehensible, Jesus is being left out of the picture resulting in the meaning of life being misunderstood. An eternal utopia of sameness would be a description of Jesus being left out of the picture, because a universe filled with only dark matter and nothing would be boring and expected.

The picture below is designed to show that God does the unexpected. It would be expected for there to be only one color of light, since light is made of only one type of particle in multiple ratios of itself. It is amazing that the photon when transmitted in different ratios produces different colors of light. When the light strikes an object some of the photons are absorbed and some are transmitted back to your eyes. The picture above of Micah and Mason holding the Legos is designed to show that God does the unexpected. Could the reader make an airplane or car like the one the boys are holding in their left hands out of one type of Lego as Mason demonstrates with the blue Legos and Micah with the white?

Madelyn dressed in one color and Melody in multi colored clothes.

Micah and Mason hold a model in their right hand made from one type of lego. In their left hand they hold a model made from different legos.

(From left to right, Madelyn is dressed in one color and Melody in multi colored clothes. Also, Micah and Mason build what they can out of one Lego held in their right hand and hold a model made from different Legos in their left hand.)

The detail, diversity, and functionality of the product would be expected to be minimal. God does the unexpected and creates substances or things that appear to be distinctly different like the airplane and car using one universal building block. It is amazing and truly unexpected that both are made of the same singular building block according to an infinite universe in the total existence theory.

As treasure seekers, we want to understand "The Truth" in order to make the best products and understand the laws by which we are governed. As we seek the truth to a problem it concerns seeking perfection in the task at hand. What is truth? It is the correct answer to the problem. Any government built on an imperfect foundation will not last. The Genesis account of Creation is founded on this principle. Adam and Eve in this account were created sinless, which means that they understood the difference between what is good and what is bad. An insane animal does not know the difference. Adults can't blame apes which are insane as the reason a crime occurred in court, because they would be implying equality; since science has proven that some behaviors are learned and some are inherited. If humans randomly evolved from apes, then the majority would still have the inherited insanity behavior and establishing a justice system would be dubious. An adult could easily argue that Homo sapiens have not existed on Earth long enough for these genes to have all become recessive.

The Bible states that after creating Adam and giving him a garden to protect and tend, God made a covenant of works with him as the representative of humanity (Gen. 2:15-17). Living in the garden, Adam endured a period of testing. He was good but not perfect, and if he had obeyed the Lord, he would have earned a perfect righteousness before the Creator. Yet Adam was also able to disobey God and lose favor with Him. The test Adam faced involved the Tree of Knowledge of Good and Evil (Gen. 2:17). Only this tree was off limits to our first parents, and had Adam not eaten of it, he would have demonstrated his trust and love for God. Before eating the forbidden fruit, Adam and Eve had a basic knowledge of good and evil.

The serpent's test is only a test because our first parents knew it was good to obey the Lord and evil to violate His will. It did not tempt them with mere knowledge of good and evil; rather, the snake said eating the fruit would make them "like God, knowing good and evil" (v. 5). In other words, they were tempted to become like the Most High, an independent agent above whom there is no law. The temptation was for Adam and Eve to deny the sufficiency of God's commands—to reach out as autonomous individuals and eat the fruit as if they were subject to no higher law. Adam and Eve were tempted to believe they were, and should be, independent of God, a law unto themselves. The idea that we can be autonomous and shake our fists in the face of God without suffering consequences is a bold-faced lie. We have no right to question what our Lord tells us is right and wrong. Therefore, Adam and Eve were cursed with difficulty in work (Gen. 3:17-18), hardship in childbirth (v. 16), and death (v. 19), and they were barred from the Tree of Life (vv. 22-24) when they ate of the forbidden tree.

Physical death did not come immediately, however. God showed Adam and Eve grace in that He delayed the arrival of death so that they might find repentance, killing an animal and clothing them (v. 21). This event anticipates the day when the Son of God would die so that His people could be clothed with Christ's righteousness. Right after Adam's failure, God was already graciously working to reconcile the world to Himself. http://www.ligonier.org/learn/devotionals/covenant-works-part/ When Eve ate from the forbidden tree she was stealing from God. What was she stealing? The forbidden tree has many characteristics and one of them would be to become like the Most High, an independent agent above whom there is no law. However, Adam and Eve did not have anyone else around at the time for them to have a desire to be worshiped by others. Remember only man is created in the image of God. In order to have a desire to be an independent agent above whom there is no law; one must realize that there would be other people that would not have this power and therefore worship them as a God. If a tree falls in a forest and no one is there to hear it fall, then who cares! The point here is why did Eve eat from the forbidden tree first; then why did Adam follow her? Eve would have had no incentive to even ask Adam to eat the fruit, if she knew that it would make her an independent God, since she could get Adam to worship her. Once Adam knew Eve ate it he would have ate it at once without being offered the fruit by Eve. Moreover Adam would have known the power she possessed by having eaten the fruit by just looking at her, since she would have exhibited an independence from him in the form of a God worthy of being worshiped.

Prior to eating the fruit, Eve lived in the Garden with Adam. Eve did not have any other competition for Adam in the form of other women looking to be with Adam. The point here is that there had to be a significant reason for Eve to do something she knew was wrong. Eve knew it was wrong to eat from the forbidden tree. What was her incentive to eat the fruit and what was her incentive to get Adam to eat the fruit as well? Life is full of desires. I desire to live on a large farm with lots of horses, cattle, and hunt animals in season. However, those desires are currently just dreams. Eve had dreams as well. She had things she wanted to accomplish, and often we desire to live within our dreams and not within our means. She wanted more than what she was given, just like I want more than what I have been given.

If we examine the law it reveals the reason Eve ate from the forbidden tree. A commandment of God is thou shall not steal. When Eve ate from the forbidden tree she was stealing from God. What was she stealing? She was stealing from God a talent that she had not been given. She wanted more, and people will often sell their souls to the devil by cheating others in order to be given a talent that does not come naturally or that was not given to them by God. We all have God given talents that are unique. Some are born with a gift that needs very little practice; while others have to practice until they recognize the gift they have been given. When Gods gifts seem easy to some, it can make it frustrating for others that have to practice to reach the full potential of the gift.

It is easier to judge the success of someone with a talent when that talent is vital for survival. If that talent makes it seem easy to do a difficult task that is vital for survival, then I would want that talent as well. For many reasons, and not just the cool factor of being able to accomplish something without any pride associated with the production of the product. Adam was given the ability to do things and did them without any pride. This is very important to understand. This is what defines a God given talent. This reason alone would drive Eve to eat from the forbidden tree.

Adam and Eve are very different from each other and God gives us talents that are unique as well. Jealousy over the perfect gifts that God gave Adam and Eve led to the desire for more which was disrespectful to God; thus the fall of Adam and Eve is a warning to us not to tell God what to do or what is best. God builds based on team work, it is amazing how he works to make so many different substances. His use of team work is a reflection of how we should be. Creating diversity in harmony with each other for the peace we all desire. Usually we get focused on how is this going to benefit me, unfortunately "Me" has no love for the team.

Matthew 22:23 is not a commandment to be good it is a commandment to love all that is good, so is homosexuality good or why do homosexuals view this lifestyle as good? Homo-sexuality is an example of a wrong biological choice, because it does not accomplish creation of the eternal spirit which sexual reproduction was designed to accomplish. Homosexuality is seen as a sin, since falling in love with yourself will make it difficult for others to love you, which in turn makes it difficult to follow the greatest commandment. Homo sapiens can't force homosexual sex to produce offspring, since the human body does not contain an asexual method of reproduction. Many plants are asexual and reproduce by budding. However earth worms contain a bisexual method of reproduction, and as hermaphrodites they use a complex biological clock to prevent inbreeding, since earth worms have the same physical appearance. The point here is to make it clear that if you were born with male anatomy, then you were born a male. Those who choose to become transsexual are no different than Adam and Eve trying to tell God what is best. Homosexuality is an ecstasy of self-love. Homosexuals are of one sexual type, which means that they are in love with their own sexuality. Homosexuals know how their body works and it is easier to please someone if you know what they desire, since Homosexuals have sex with those who have the same body type. The issue is not the sex; it is the self-love associated with the Eros making it difficult to follow the greatest commandment. We should not make it easy for people to fall in love with themselves, since those who love themselves tend to only care about themselves. This is the reason why marriage should remain as law between a man and a woman. (Matthew 22:39)

Love is displayed by the choices we make. If people were born gay, then they would not be able to demonstrate personal Love to their partner. Their personal choice to show Love to their homosexual partner would not occur, because they would be like a robot or drone unable to make an independent choice representative of personal love or affection to their partner. Born that way means, born without the ability to show personal love or affection that is representative of their own choice. Really, do you actually believe that homosexuals are born that way? Born without the ability to love their partner based on their own decisions? Love is a choice that requires a lot of work as illustrated in the parable of the Good Samaritan. If you have homophobia, memorize Philippians 2:3 this scripture has the power for your prayer to change lives.

Why do people choose to be homosexual? Addictions result from the over indulgence in an action because the action provides comfort to the individual. Alcohol, food, tobacco, gambling, and yes sex can become addicting to anyone. When we lose our trust in other people, then it becomes much easier for a serious addiction to result. The euphoria associated with an orgasm can become the ice cream that the overweight person can't stop eating. Sex can easily become addicting, since it is easy to keep it hidden from others by keeping it in the closet. When the organs are the same it is easier to communicate to the partner where stimulation for oral sex occurs the most. The orgasm itself becomes the fulfillment, because the body is rewarded with a good feeling. This can become extremely addicting and the reason why oral sex is so appealing to the one properly receiving it. Moreover, homosexuality means love for one sexuality. In Transexuality, the mind can become so addicted to one sexuality that fuels an orgasm causing it to be convinced that a sex change would be good because the thoughts fueled the orgasm and it produced a good feeling or result. Thus the goal becomes the promotion of the good associated with the feeling and to share this good with other people. The transsexual knows the feeling that produced the orgasm; the good feeling of the orgasm validates the sex change as good. The person who is over eating is caught up in the pleasure of the food and has no regards for the future life changing consequences. An auto mechanic who chooses to become a transsexual will face major life changing consequences when he reveals his decision to his fellow workers. Jennifer Chavez, 55, has 40 years of experience in the auto industry but said she was terminated from her job as a mechanic just two months after telling her boss she planned to transition from male to female. Upon finding out about her transition, she said co-workers stopped talking to her and her boss even told her an applicant had turned down a job because of her. Soon, word about her transition spread. "Prior to my transition, getting a job was nothing," said Chavez. "After my transition, a huge segment of Atlanta in the auto service world knew about me, so I was blackballed from all the auto dealerships."

More than 300 applications later, she landed a full-time, commission-based technician job at Pep Boys, where her potential annual earnings are around $35,000—half of what she previously made. As a result, she has barely been able to hold on to her home.

—See more at: http://money.cnn.com/2013/02/22/pf/transgender-unemployment/index.html Moreover, the person who is gambling at the casino with stolen money from their workplace is caught up in the pleasure of the good that money can buy with no regards for the future life changing consequences of a bad bet. Fame and the desire for more immediate gratification with an award for being the best can produce the workaholic whom is in the same paragraph as the homosexuals and the transgenders. Only through the truth, whom Jesus Christ has revealed to us by the power of his Holy Spirit can the workaholic change his ways because he now understands the meaning of life. Before the workaholic lived for the thrill associated with the gratifications of the flesh which are meaningless and soon to be forgotten; this is the reality that the addict refuses to accept. The now is defined by the Love that Jesus has for your spirit and your choice to follow Matthew 22:37.

Our justice system blatantly affirms the stance that humans did not come from an insane animal, thus they can't be blamed for our behavior. Moreover, if we did evolve randomly from an insane animal, then this could be used as an explanation for violent or evil behavior and be considered normal! It is not normal for a young man to go and kill an older man and take his territory. Animals in the wild are known to kill and rape over territory with no repercussions. Therefore the principles of human evolution from an insane species would require a virgin birth of Adam and Eve for the establishment of a moral and just human government. (Isaiah 9:6)

Jesus said," The truth will set you free." The truth sets us free from worry. (John 3:16) The author aims to promote freedom through the life of Jesus Christ. Anything less than the pursuit of perfection in the products we produce would be unpatriotic to the men and women that sacrificed their lives for this country. Thus united we stand in the pursuit of perfection.

As a Christian, my purpose is to prepare the way for the return of our lord and savior Jesus Christ. The word is the power to make your spirit eternal. God is eternal, the question is do you believe that he can make your spirit which is a creation of God eternal? You do not have the knowledge to make your spirit eternal alone, thus trying to find the way to make your spirit eternal alone would be like trying to fly an airplane blind. Jews, Muslims, and rest of the world we are to get them ready, since even Thomas a disciple of Jesus doubted that he had truly risen from the grave and had to see him in the flesh to believe. (John 20:24-29) The point here is that if the way is not prepared, then many will chose not to believe even if they see Jesus in the flesh. I see many people every day and do not believe everything that they say. It is a choice to believe what Jesus says. He will not force you into Hell, the Devil will come and get his servants.

If you ask most religious scholars why the world is corrupt they will say because of the fall of Adam and Eve. Adam and Eve are to blame! The chosen in heaven don't blame Adam and Eve, since Jesus accepted blame for all sin. The devil has no dominion in heaven and can't be blamed in heaven for the choices we made on Earth, because of free will. Why? Jesus Christ is a representation of how good is stronger than evil, since good can support any burden that evil can bring to bear, for example what did Judas do when he was to blame for giving Jesus over to be crucified? Judas Iscariot could not handle the sin that he was blamed for and he killed himself, spiritual destruction follows the same path. Very often in life our sin is exposed and the grief is overwhelming and forgiveness seems out of reach. This is the reason Jesus chose to do what he did, there was no other way. Jesus spoke to us in parables, so that we would have to reason out the truth. Christ puts us to the test to see if we will deny the truth. When we deny the truth we deny Jesus Christ. He is fully aware of our intentions.

When a farmer goes to a vine, he will care for a vine that produces a crop. A farmer loves the plant that produces a gorgeous crop; he will ignore a plant that does not produce a crop and eventually remove it, since that plant is not working for the farmer. How do you produce a crop?

The call to prepare the way concerns teaching others without fear about the truth. Do not fear the truth. Do you care more about what others think than you care about the truth? (John 12:43) Jesus is the farmer and he prunes the followers that produce the crops. Did Jesus come to abolish the law or fulfil it? If Christianity is the only way to heaven, then he came to abolish the law. Christianity being the only way would be the new law. Telling a new Christian that they are saved by Grace and not informing them that they are still accountable to The Greatest Commandment would establish a new law. (Matthew 5:17)

People get ready Jesus is coming. Get ready means the people have to have a love for God in order for grace to be given. If you doubt this, then why does the preacher make the call at the end of the sermon to come forward, publicly acknowledge Jesus as your lord and savior and be baptized? Unfortunately, grace is being offered before people are ready and this is the reason abortion is legal in this country. Our God is a God of the living and not of the dead, thus he has no plan to create nothing or become it. (Luke 20:38) In our God the creator of our Lord Jesus Christ, time has no beginning or end. Whose Son is the Christ? David thus calls him Lord, so how is he his son? (Luke 20:41-44) Jesus healed many people, so he had the power to speak to the body. If the spirit is weaker than the body, don't expect the body to follow the commands of its own spirit. (John 18:6) Sin hurts other people, thus we should be held accountable or blamed for the pain we caused others. However, just like Judas we are not strong enough to carry that burden. Jesus sets us free from this burden or the pain and blame others point at us because we hurt them with our sin. The finger was pointed to Jesus at Calvary.

The Holy Trinity is composed of the Father, Son, and Holy Spirit. When a new believer is baptized, they receive the gift of the Holy Spirit. Why is this important? Trying to forgive someone who he sinned against you without the Holy Spirit would be like trying to pass a camel through the eye of a needle. Without the Holy Spirit and eye for an eye prevails and it becomes impossible to love your neighbor as Jesus defines the neighbor in the New Testament.

The kingdom of Heaven is within us in the form of a Trinity. In Matthew 13:18-23 Jesus speaks of a parable about a farmer and the seed. The seed that fell on the footpath and was trampled represents those that ignore the love God offers and the evil one comes snatches the message from their Hearts. Every person upon their creation has the love of God planted as a seed in their Heart. The seed that falls on the rocky soil represents those who have the love of God in their Mind only; they gladly hear the message and accept it right away. As soon as life gets hard or decisions get hard, they give up. The seed that fell among the thorns represents those who have the love of God in their soul and mind. This represents those who hear the message, which means the love is in their mind. However, their soul leads their mind to worries about the needs of this life and is fooled by the desire to get rich. The mind is only a decision maker. The seed that fell on the good soil are the people who hear the message given to the Soul through the Holy Spirit and make a decision with their Mind through the passion of their Heart to act and produce a crop as much as a hundred or sixty or thirty times what was originally given.

When Jesus became sin, we are acknowledging that he took on our sin or accepted blame for it and was punished on the Cross for our sin. Why would he do that? Love... God knows we could not handle the punishment required for our sin. Rules were not followed for an honorable sacrifice, thus God was put to the test. Jesus was a circumcised Jew, however the Jews rejected him so he did not fall under the protection of Jewish law. Jewish law had a maximum of 40 lashes. If the flogged person died after the 40, the one who whipped him could be found guilty of manslaughter since punishment was intended, not execution. Therefore, wisdom prevailed and 39 lashes was the norm. The Jewish whip was made of three straps of leather from three different species and 13 blows were landed to deliver a total of 39 stripes. This is per Edersheim, the Messianic (Christian) Jewish author from the late 1800's. According to the Roman proconsul the number of lashes was unlimited. The Roman soldiers faced no consequence for over lashing Jesus, so what stopped the lashing? Yes, it's possible that muscle fatigue stopped the lashings by the Roman soldiers. The Bible does not say how many times Jesus was lashed, yet he survived six hours nailed to a cross. His Love is truly inspirational, because it is so unexpected! When the word became flesh, God put to the test those who said they believe the word. Jesus didn't tell Peter what to do and that might lead some to think that Jesus was a poor communicator. The Jews did not expect Jesus to rise from the grave and to this day they do not believe. It could easily be concluded that what Jesus did on the cross was too nice for us. People walk all over those who are kind or soft, so was Jesus naïve? Often followers of Christ will say that the world is corrupt because of the sin in the world and that the devil has been given the authority to rule over Earth. Satan is the major influence on the ideals, opinions, goals, hopes and views of the majority of people. His influence also encompasses the world's philosophies, education, and commerce. Money drives this world and the choices made do not reflect as it is in Heaven, the rich young ruler struggled with the idea of being on the same financial class as the gentiles.

What does the Lord's prayer state? Is the Lord's Prayer naïve? Jesus makes it clear that we can have Heaven on Earth if we chose to!

Peter denied knowing Jesus three times, because he was not a man of prayer. Peter did not know how to pray, because he did not understand what it took to make his prayers work. (Matthew 26:40) Peter was not a master of Philippian's 2:3 which states do nothing out of selfish ambition or vain conceit, but in humility consider others better than yourselves. The disciples asked Jesus how to pray and he provided the Lord's Prayer. The point here is that when you pray God knows the motives of your heart, soul and mind. (Philippians 2:3)

Who was the greatest man to have ever been born out of a mother's womb or the greatest man to have ever lived? Jesus is the Son of God, so the obvious answer would be Jesus. However, Jesus says that John the Baptist was the greatest. Jesus was not a liar, so why did he say the John the Baptist was greater than the Christ born of a virgin womb? John the Baptist is associated with loving God, since he prepared the way for Grace. If you are a Christian and you think that Grace is above the greatest commandment you are wrong. Jesus did not forgive Satan for his sin, because he does not love God. Don't take my word for it, read Luke 7:28 and Matthew 7:21-23. What is written in the law points out the opposites that exist and the choices associated with them. In Luke 10:25-28 Jesus makes it clear that even those who love God the least in the Kingdom of God is greater. Talk about humility that is remarkable humility by Jesus Christ. Jesus is associated with Grace; one can only get to heaven through the son. This fact alone should make Jesus the Greatest man to have ever come from a mother's womb, however Luke 7:28 can't be overruled.

John the Baptist condemned Herod to Hell for being an adulator, since he had no desire to change his ways and Love God. (Mark 6:14-29) John the Baptist is associated with loving God, since he prepared the way for Grace. Why does this matter? John the Baptist got his head cut off for speaking the truth about consequences. It is obvious that Herod used his position as King to do whatever he wanted with complete disregard to God's Word. That is why John rebuked King Herod! Herod was sinful and unrepentant for his actions. If a preacher tells his congregation that all they need to do is accept Jesus and be saved by Grace without informing them of the consequences of not being born again, then why should they have any regard to God's word? John the Baptist was not afraid to speak the truth about the importance of loving God. Money made Herod appear to have authority. How much authority does he have now?

Baptism is associated with accepting Jesus and being saved by grace. Being saved by grace means you should have received a punishment for your sin which hurt other people. The problem is that Grace tends to be put above The Greatest Commandment Matthew 22:37. If Grace were above the Greatest Commandment, then the devil could be forgiven and he would be in heaven. The devil does not love God and this is the reason he is not in heaven. The purpose of following the law is to show others that we love God. Unfortunately, those that view grace above the greatest commandment are using the law as a means to judge others as being not good enough to follow it. This is the common argument against the Jew.

Love or judge, the choice is yours! Matthew 22:37 states you are called to Love and the law tell us how. Not knowing that God loves us is associated with our inherited sin from the fall of Adam and Eve as evidence in the promotion of an incomprehensible God by both secular and religious organizations. To not accept that God is comprehendible at his core represents evidence of inherited sin, and if you follow the Devil he will destroy you as stated in Matthew 10:28. The goal of the devil is to promote Jesus as incomprehensible, since he chose to not accept the power and riches of this world as stated in Matthew 4:8-9. Most live their life in the pursuit of material wealth or power over people. This is the primary reason people buy lottery tickets.

Was Jesus incomprehensible to reject the offer of wealth and power? The Devil would like for you to think that is the truth. Wealth and power create what is commonly referred to as a nut cracker. Only when you believe in Jesus should you be baptized. Those who are baptized are called to prepare the way like John the Baptist. This is not easy to do because most judge success by monetary means. What should the church look like? How did Jesus rule the church when he was here on Earth? The Church is the body of believers as stated in Matthew 17:4. For God so loved the world that he sent his son not to condemn the world but to save it. Christ forgives our old sinful ways, since being born again is associated with a change in behavior because we now see that God loves us and therefore we now desire to love him.

If grace is infinite, then it would not be a choice to love God. If grace is infinite, there would be no reason to change our ways and become a new creation or be born again. If grace is infinite, then God would accept evil and thus be evil. To forgive and not expect any change in behavior would produce more of the same behavior that the original forgiveness required. The point here is that God does not require us to be good, He does require us to Love all that is good.

Chapter 2

Total Existence Theory

Everything that we see is a shadow cast by that which we do not see.

Martin Luther King, Jr

O ur universe is either finite or infinite. Universe is the totality of all the things that exist, so there is only one Universe and the question is whether it is finite or infinite? The objective is to clarify the differences between the two possibilities, since the belief in God is defined by description. The Total Existence Theory compares the finite universe to the infinite universe and allows the reader to make a choice based on the educated conclusions presented. The theory is defined as the Total Existence Theory, since the Universe is either infinite or finite and a theory attempts to educate others concerning conclusions based on evidence.

There is much evidence being promoted by the scientific community about the finite universe or Big Bang Theory. It is not the writer's intent to come up with a theory opposite of the Big Bang Theory, since it needs to be included in the Total Existence Theory because of free will and the importance of choice. Moreover, it is very difficult to understand a concept without comparing it to something opposite or different. Fundamentally, the writer has no desire to force anyone to believe that the universe is infinite. Promotion in the scientific community is no different than the religious community in that if you do not believe what the people at the top believe, then you will not be promoted.

Preventing others from knowing all the possibilities does not promote choice and freedom which this country is founded upon. If it is ever proven to be finite or infinite, then the Total Existence Theory would no longer be a theory requiring belief and the universe would be defined by law as finite or infinite and the description of God would no longer require belief. Both models of the current universe will be defined as follows: big bang theory and steady state theory described. According to the Big Bang theory will the Higgs Boson or God particle ever be destroyed or changed into nothing?

If the God particle is changed into nothing, then God would be proven to be both something and nothing and belief in his description would no longer be required! Colossians 1:15-17 states God is present with us and not off somewhere in the distance as the all mighty uncomprehend able blend of something and nothing. If God created something from nothing, then both something and nothing would be a part of him. The problem is that something and nothing are total opposites. Nothing is associated with no movement, something is associated with movement and to be both would mean opposites do not exist and that truth over a long period of time will become a lie. Truth and lies are never interchangeable and will always be opposites as stated in Isaiah 40:8, 1 Peter1:25, and Matthew 24:35.

Comparing Matthew 24:35 to John 3:16 reveals that our spirit is the only thing in the Universe that is truly similar in structure to our God and his word. If our spirit is not eternal, then 10^{150} years in heaven would seem like a blink of the eye compared to eternity. Time is relative to what one gets accustom to in the surroundings. Matthew 24:35 makes no mention of hell passing away, thus accountability is still being addressed.

According to the Big Bang opposites do not exist, because nothing created something and something will eventually turn back into nothing. Things that are finite have a birth and a death. *Thus according to the Big Bang a truth will eventually turn into a lie, because it states that emptiness, nothing, and something are all interchangeable and equal making miracles an illusion or lie.* A theory for everything is only possible if opposites do not exist. If God created something from nothing, he would not be a jealous God because he could easily turn something back into nothing and God would be everything. The point here is that no scripture in the Bible specifically states that God created something from nothing. (John 5:17)

Is the Big Bang really a scientific theory? What is emptiness? Can a test be used to confirm its existence? Emptiness is the absence of time, space, matter, and energy. http://www.allaboutscience.org/big-bang-theory.htm So what would be used to test for its existence? Emptiness is an imaginary or fictitious concept, and for nothing to appear out of it is not possible to comprehend. It would not be a miracle, because the finite universe does not promote opposites. The finite universe promotes God as everything, thus opposites do not exist. Emptiness, nothing, and something are all interchangeable, thus they are not opposites. Good and evil would be the same and everyone would go to heaven or hell, since there are no opposites in the finite universe.

First of all, it is not really known whether or not the universe started from a singularity. Our measurements can take us back only so far; ideas about the nature of the cosmos at the start of the big bang are mostly unproved conjecture. (http://www.scientificamerican.com/article.cfm?id=according-to-the-big-bang)

A miracle is a record that an unprovable opposite has occurred. Miracles could be considered evidence other than math (zero does not equal one) that opposites are a part of the Universe and that our Universe is Infinite.

Mgr. Georges Lemaître, a Belgian priest-astronomer and known as "the father of modern cosmology" first proposed the Big Bang theory. According to Crawley, he showed unusual intellectual precocity as a child and decided aged 10 that he wanted to become a Catholic priest. After fighting in the Great War he was ordained in Belgium in 1923—and a month later came over to St Edmund's, Cambridge, to study for a doctorate. Then, after further study at Harvard and MIT, he became professor of physics at Louvain University in Belgium, where he remained until his death in 1966.

Mgr. Lemaître was not happy with Pope Pius XII's belief that the book of Genesis had been vindicated by his cosmological discoveries, and that "Fiat Lux!" ("Let there be light!") coincided with his Big Bang theory. This was not because he rejected Genesis but because he felt the two disciplines, theology and science, should be studied separately without requiring mutual confirmation.

David T. Steineker

http://www.catholicherald.co.uk/commentandblogs/2012/10/03/the-belgian-priest-who-invented-the-big-bang-theory-shows-up-the-canard-about-faith-and-science/

Georges Lemaître first proposed what became the Big Bang theory in what he called his "hypothesis of the primeval atom." Over time, scientists built on his initial ideas to form the modern synthesis. The framework for the Big Bang model relies on Albert Einstein's general relativity and on simplifying assumptions such as homogeneity and isotropy of space. The governing equations had been formulated by Alexander Friedmann. In 1929, Edwin Hubble discovered that the distances to far away galaxies were generally proportional to their redshifts—an idea originally suggested by Lemaître in 1927. Hubble's observation was taken to indicate that all very distant galaxies and clusters have an apparent velocity directly away from our vantage point: the farther away, the higher the apparent velocity. Independently deriving Friedmann's equations in 1927, Georges Lemaître, a Belgian physicist and Roman Catholic priest, proposed that the inferred recession of the nebulae was due to the expansion of the Universe. Independently deriving Friedmann's equations in 1927, Georges Lemaître, a Belgian physicist and Roman Catholic priest, proposed that the inferred recession of the nebulae was due to the expansion of the Universe.

In 1931 Lemaître went further and suggested that the evident expansion of the universe, if projected back in time, meant that the further in the past the smaller the universe was, until at some finite time in the past all the mass of the Universe was concentrated into a single point, a "primeval atom" where and when the fabric of time and space came into existence. Lemaître, thought that if the world has begun with a single quantum, the notions of space and time would altogether fail to have any meaning at the beginning; they would only begin to have a sensible meaning when the original quantum had been divided into a sufficient number of quanta. If this suggestion is correct, the beginning of the world happened a little before the beginning of space and time. The beginning of the world in this description is associated with the formation of matter from nothing; then the beginning of space and time follow.

It is important to note that the Big Bang occurred everywhere at once. http://spaceplace.nasa.gov/review/dr-marc-space/center-of-universe.html Why does this matter? Nothing did not produce something from one point and continue the expansion! A finite universe should have one point of origin, and an Infinite Universe should lack a point of origin. This is more evidence that the universe is infinite. The conditions needed for this to occur everywhere at once are not comprehendible. These statements are the requirements for a linear view of time, since the linear view of time concerns the Earth moving around the Sun with the age of the Earth at 4.5 billion years or rotations around the sun. The universe is defined by the big bang as 13.77 billion years old or 13.77 billion earth rotations around our sun to promote a linear past, present, and future view of time.

Peter led the church with aggression and promoted compassion because of Colossians 1:15. Peter was not afraid to live, because he knew others would be inspired by his compassion. Peter requested to be crucified upside down and embraced death to promote truth. Virtuous and honorable are words that define Peter. In an infinite universe, Jesus is the first born of all creation just like God is the alpha and omega of all creation. The infinite universe makes it possible for Jesus to be the first born of all creation and to have left heaven and to have come to Earth two thousand years ago.

In the '50s, Pope Pious XII stated that the big bang theory affirmed the idea of a creator and was in line with Christian beliefs, leaving some to associate steady-state theory with atheism [source: American Institute of Physics]. The church has a role to promote the truth, since accountability and the meaning of life are tied to it. Jesus put Peter to the test, so God has a purpose associated with when his truth is revealed. Moreover, the author takes no claim to the truth that God reveals to his creation, since a genius is a foolish prophet. (Philippians 2:3)

Saint Peter did not have the authority to deny other disciples communion at the Lord's Table. (Luke 9:49-50, Mark 9:38-41) The intentions of the author are to convince the Catholic Church to offer communion to all believers, since John the Baptist would not have consumed the wine at the last supper. Jesus washed the disciple's feet, do you not think that Peter would do likewise? Washing someone's feet is an act of humility. The leader must be seen as humble in order for their prayers to produce results. (Philippians 2:3) The author would encourage the Catholic Church to offer both wine and juice since wine can cause some believers like Samson to become weak. (Luke 9:49-50, Mark 9:38-41) Furthermore, the goal is to strengthen the church that Jesus Christ stated would be built on Peter the rock. Peter was a handsome man, since he was noticed by three different people before the roster crowed during the morning of the crucifixion.

When Jesus rose from the dead, he asked Peter three times if he loved him. Jesus wanted Peter to understand the significance of betrayal. Those who are handsome often lose sight of what is important, because they get caught up in the praise of men being more satisfying than the praise of God. David struggled with this and Bathsheba is the evidence. Moreover, in the '50s, Pope Pious XII stated that the big bang theory affirmed the idea of a creator and was in line with Christian beliefs.

In cosmology, the Steady State theory (also known as the Infinite Universe theory or continuous creation) is a model developed as an alternative to the Big Bang theory (the standard cosmological model). In steady state views, new matter is continuously created as the universe expands, so that the perfect cosmological principle is adhered to. The steady state model is now largely discredited, as the observational evidence points to a Big Bang-type cosmology and a finite age of the universe.

The author notes here that the steady State theory is not a correct definition of an Infinite Universe, since it states new matter is continuously created as the universe expands. Infinity is defined as the difference between zero and one, so an infinite universe requires something and nothing to be unchangeable. The Steady State theory is being described here along with the big bang theory, so that the reader can be educated concerning the current definition of both theories. The goal of the writer is to present challenges to these theories, so that the reader can make an educated decision about the totality existence theory. Furthermore, an infinite universe lacks a beginning, so there is no one set past or a given future. Zero divided by one proves that something will divide into nothing zero times. Something (1) will go into nothing (0) a total of zero times, thus (0/1=0). What does this mean? When we talk about using numbers in ratios, for example (1/2) or 1 meter divided by two meters (only half of 2 meters will fit into 1 meter).

Numbers are meaningless unless they have units associated with them, like meter is associated with length. The one and the two are defined by dimensions. "Something", which has dimension, will fit into "Nothing", which has no dimension zero times, because "Something" is too big to fit into "Nothing". Therefore, do not view "Something" as being small in nature! This proves that something in its pure sense cannot change into nothing in the absolute sense. Moreover, the one and zero are separate and distinct.

A calculator will read error when (1 / 0) is computed, since "Nothing" cannot divide "Something". Therefore, how many times could nothing fit into something? The answer is not infinite, since a true number for the answer does not exist. This means we could count infinitely and never reach the correct number. An infinite amount of nothing is still zero. Is the answer zero, like (0/1=0)? The answer can't be zero, because something is larger than nothing. Furthermore, when (1/0) is calculated these are the reasons error is given as the answer. Something must at all times be larger than nothing in order for (1/0) to be an error. Our universe is either finite or infinite. It can't be both, because either zero is equal to one or zero is not equal to one. The objective is to further clarify the differences between the two possibilities.

Proposed in 1948 by Hermann Bondi, Thomas Gold, and Fred Hoyle, the steady-state theory was based on an extension of something called the perfect cosmological principle. This holds that the universe looks essentially the same from every spot in it and at every time. The steady-state theory began to wither in the 1960s. First, astronomers discovered quasars, the highly luminous cores of very distant galaxies. Because the vast majority of quasars lie exceedingly far away, their existence proves that the perfect cosmological principle cannot be true—the distant and therefore ancient universe is not the same as the younger universe nearby. The death knell for the theory sounded when radio astronomers Arno Penzias and Robert Wilson discovered the cosmic microwave background, the leftover radiation from the Big Bang. The steady-staters had no reasonable way to explain this radiation, and their theory slowly faded away as so many of its predecessors had. http://www.pbs.org/wnet/hawking/universes/html/univ_steady.html

Tommy Gold's idea, inspired by the British horror film the dead night, was that as the universe expanded new matter was created in the widening gaps between the galaxies. The idea that the universe is always changing yet remains the same is called dynamic equilibrium. Although the theory does not explain how matter could be created from nothing, the same criticism could be leveled at the Big Bang theory.

The two competing theories were now established: The Big Bang theory predicted that the universe is expanding from a single point and that the remnants of the Big Bang could be observed in the form of microwaves. The Steady State theory proposed that although the universe is expanding, new matter is always being created so that the average density of matter in the universe does not change. The rate of matter creation needed (~ 10^{-9} atoms m^{-3} yr^{-1}) was very small and could not be ruled out experimentally. The Steady State theory predicted that no microwave signal would be observed. But neither theory was perfect. http://cosmology.carnegiescience.edu/timeline/1949/gold-bondi-hoyle

According to the finite view of the universe, the Big Bang occurred approximately 13.77 billion years ago, which is thus considered the age of the universe. After this time, the Universe was in an extremely hot and dense state and began expanding rapidly. After the initial expansion, the Universe cooled sufficiently to allow energy to be converted into various subatomic particles, including protons, neutrons, and electrons. The Big Bang is not an explosion of matter moving outward to fill an empty universe. Instead, space itself expands with time everywhere and increases the physical distance between two moving points. Though simple atomic nuclei could have formed quickly, thousands of years were needed before the appearance of the first electrically neutral atoms.

The first element produced was hydrogen, along with traces of helium and lithium. Giant clouds of these primordial elements later coalesced through gravity to form stars and galaxies, and the heavier elements were synthesized either within stars or during supernovae. The Big Bang is considered a well-tested scientific theory and is widely accepted within the scientific community.

It offers a comprehensive explanation for a broad range of observed phenomena, including the abundance of light elements, the cosmic microwave background, large scale structure, and the Hubble diagram for Type IA supernovae. The core ideas of the Big Bang—the expansion, the early hot state, the formation of helium, and the formation of galaxies— are derived from these and other observations that are independent of any cosmological model. As the distance between galaxy clusters is increasing today, it is inferred that everything was closer together in the past. This idea has been considered in detail back in time to extreme densities and temperatures, and large particle accelerators have been built to experiment in such conditions, resulting in further development of the model. On the other hand, these accelerators have limited capabilities to probe into such high energy regimes.

There is little evidence regarding the absolute earliest instant of the expansion.

Thus, the Big Bang theory cannot and does not provide any explanation for such an initial condition; rather, it describes and explains the general evolution of the universe going forward from that point on. The total existence theory defines both the finite universe and the infinite universe and provides the reader with the facts so that they can make their own educated conclusion.

- FINITE UNIVERSE—zero and one are equal, therefore matter can be infinitely divided into nothing—(God is "Nothing" that created everything out of emptiness) At the Planck distance and the Planck time all physics, as we know it today collapses. This is the reason we call the beginning of the big bang a singularity. You cannot apply ordinary reasoning there. Zero and one have no sense there.(www.BigBang.org) The Big Bang theory is evidence for a mathematical proof defining zero and one as equal. Currently, math and physics before the Big Bang and after it do not relate. "Something" can't just forget where it came from! Why should this spectacular random singularity be left out of current proofs, since it is such an important event? It is not that it is a singularity, it is a random singularity. This is the reason no end date to the Universe has ever been given. This theory that nothing created everything including the singularity that caused the big bang works well for Atheists, since they believe that nothing is in control and some Creationists agree with the idea that God created everything. However, considering that it defines God as "Nothing" they aren't promoting it in church. Nothing and Emptiness are not the same; according to this universe nothing has power over emptiness, since nothing created everything out of emptiness. Emptiness is proven not to exist based on its own definition. Emptiness is the absence of space, time, matter, and energy, thus no test can be done to validate its existence. It is common knowledge that substances which are finite have predictable endings. To even begin to publicly claim that the Universe was finite without being able to give a predictable ending shows a lack of self-discipline and general education.

According to Steven Hawking, a big bang physicist a finite Universe is capable of multiple spontaneous creations, thus producing additional new space, energy, and matter into the Finite Universe providing evidence for a mathematical proof justifying 0=1. The point here is that God being defined without comprehension leads to justification for sin. Moreover God can't be understood, so it's not my fault that I sin.

Life does not commonly arise from nonliving elements, thus a spontaneous generation of life would be considered a singularity or miracle and be defined as an opposite of the expected outcome. Getting life from nonliving elements is complicated since genetic information requires a sequence of events. If everything is the result of randomness, then why doesn't the percent abundance of isotopes of atoms constantly change in percent? Carbon has 3 isotopes, carbon-12 (98.9% abundant), carbon-13 (1.1% abundant), carbon-14 (less than 0.1% abundant), and the percent's of the three don't randomly change over time. They are the same percent's, and this allows us to date or tell how old a substance is on Earth, by using radioactive decay or carbon dating. Moreover, if Carbon's percent abundance changed randomly from carbon-12 (98.9% abundant) to 69% abundant, then its Molar mass on the periodic table would change. If you are closest to twelve in mass, then your mass will represent this fact on the periodic table. The most remarkable observation about the periodic table concerns this point, since it is not expected.

The ratio (1/any whole number) is the reason why most scientists believe that nothing formed something. Why? As the number in the denominator increases the answer becomes smaller. The question becomes when is so so so small so so so close to nothing? Most scientists are estimators; look at the rules of significant digits. Something has been estimated to equal zero after numerous divisions.

Could God have no mass and be a creator that only moves? This possibility leads to some questions. How would God distinguish between spirits in Heaven? How could a God with no mass be perfect, since he would lack a force of attraction and would be void of substance? In Matthew 17:1-13, Mark 9:2-13, and Luke 9:28-36 descriptions of the transfiguration of Jesus are given. These accounts are important; because they clearly show a visible distinction between Elijah and Moses (we see matter, because we are made of matter). Both of whom are in Heaven right now and I guarantee you that they would not consider themselves Gods separate from the God of creation. Remember Heaven is an eternal place. The question is do you believe that Jesus is God in the flesh? God is great; his perfect mass and perfect power of movement are worthy of praise. If God is a combination of something and nothing as many believe, then opposites do not exist.

In order for there to be absolute truth, it must be opposite of a lie. If the reader believes that God is a combination of something and nothing, then they believe that truth and lies are the same and that God can't be understood. The Pharisees believed that God could not be understood and this is the reason they did not believe what Jesus Christ taught. Matthew 12:23-24 states all the crowds were amazed, and were saying, "This man cannot be the Son of David, can he?" But when the Pharisees heard *this*, they said, "This man casts out demons only by Beelzebul the ruler of the demons." But be on your guard against the yeast of the Pharisees and Sadducees. Then they understood the he was not telling them to guard against the yeast used in bread, but against the teaching of the Pharisees and Sadducees (Matthew 16:11-12).

Unfortunately, many leaders in the church are still listening to the Pharisees and Sadducees due to their belief that God calls us to be good and those who are not good should be punished if not by the church then by the government. Grace promotes peace, and an eye for an eye promotes more crime. Why, then in the book of Mark did the rich young man run up to Jesus and fall on his knees and ask what must I do to inherit eternal life? Jesus did not say go and be baptized! The rich man refused to show love for God. The fear of death is associated with not knowing what lies beyond, since this world seems so predictable. It must be noted that the rich young ruler was giving 10 percent of his income to the temple, since he stated he followed all of the law.

Why is the church listening to the teaching of the Pharisees and Sadducees? When we associate ourselves with likeminded and those with similar behavior, then we can more easily build a big church or temple and encourage others to act like us. How many temple buildings did Jesus build? If you say that was not his purpose, then why do we too often associate ourselves as being successful Christians with the building that we attend? The rich man struggled with this path of self-righteousness and it lead him to choose to follow the unforgivable sin, because he could never accept himself as being seen as financially equal to the homosexuals or gentiles. Understanding God is important, since belief leads to action in the decisions that are made.

To prove the big bang researchers have invested heavily in particle accelerators. These accelerators cool particles then smash them. The particle they are trying to destroy or change into nothing is called the God particle http://ngm. nationalgeographic.com/2008/03/god-particle/achenbach-text.

When atomic nuclei smash together, the goal is to examine the exotic particles that result. Like dismantling a car engine to figure out how it works. The Higgs Boson or God particle is the missing evidence in a theory that explains how fundamental particles acquire mass. The plan is to try and smash the God particle apart creating energies and temperatures not seen since the universe's earliest moments, then determine how it fits back together is the goal. If nothing can produce something at any moment in the Universe, then that Universe is Finite and its future will require the something returning to nothing producing a mathematical proof of 0=1.

Moreover, in a finite universe opposites do not exist and miracles are impossible, since it is an illusion that something and nothing are different.

If you don't know where you come from, then you have no idea where you are going. "Nothing" can't deny its creative character, if it can produce something; nor can it deny its destructive character when it returns something to nothing, therefore something can't just forget where it came from. It would be imbedded into its basic structure, thus 0=1. There are generally considered to be three outstanding problems with the Big Bang theory: the horizon problem, the flatness problem, and the magnetic monopole problem. The most common answer to these problems is inflationary theory; however, since this creates new problems, other options have been proposed, such as the Weyl curvature hypothesis.

A finite universe will have a death, since it is not eternal. So, how is it predicted to end? The Big Rip: 20+ billion years from now is possible only if the energy density of dark energy actually increases without limit over time. Such dark energy is called phantom energy and is unlike any known kind of energy. In this case, the expansion rate of the universe will increase without limit. Gravitationally bound systems, such as clusters of galaxies, galaxies, and ultimately the Solar System will be torn apart. The Big Crunch: 100+ billion years from now requires dark energy to be negative and the universe to be closed, then it would be possible that the expansion of the universe would reverse and the universe would contract towards a hot, dense state. The Big freeze: 10^{14} years and beyond is generally considered to be the most likely, as it occurs if the universe continues expanding as it has been. Over a time scale on the order of 10^{14} years or less, existing stars burn out, stars cease to be created, and the universe goes dark. Over a much longer time scale in the eras following this, the galaxy evaporates as the stellar remnants comprising it escape into space, and black holes evaporate.

The Heat death: 10^{150}+ years from now is a possible final state of the universe, estimated at after 10^{150} years, in which it has "run down" to a state of no thermodynamic free energy to sustain motion or life. In physical terms, it has reached maximum entropy (because of this, the term "entropy" has often been confused with Heat Death, to the point of entropy being labelled as the "force killing the universe"). The hypothesis of a universal heat death stems from the 1850s ideas of William Thomson (Lord Kelvin) who extrapolated the theory of heat views of mechanical energy loss in nature, as embodied in the first two laws of thermodynamics, to universal operation.

- INFINITE UNIVERSE—zero is not equal to one, thus there is a point where matter can't be divided—(God is "Something" that can neither be created nor destroyed that is dependent on "Nothing") In all other cases, Newton used the phenomenon of motion to explain the origin of various forces acting on bodies, but in the case of gravity, he was unable to experimentally identify the motion that produces the force of gravity. Moreover, he refused to even offer a hypothesis as to the cause of this force on grounds that to do so was contrary to sound science. He lamented that "philosophers have hitherto attempted the search of nature in vain" for the source of the gravitational force, as he was convinced "by many reasons" that there were "causes hitherto unknown" that were fundamental to all the "phenomena of nature". These fundamental phenomena are still under investigation and, though hypotheses abound, the definitive answer is yet to be found.

Gravity is a force that lacks activation, since it is constant and the only way that we know of to produce gravitons uniformly from a surface is to make that surface have a lot of mass! Moreover, Newton's second law states that an object must have mass in order to produce a force. Why is gravity being used as evidence for this universe? The infinite Universe supports the view that all particles considered to be energy have mass or substance; that there is one fundamental particle which accounts for all the diverse forms of matter in the Universe. It is the ultimate example of team work, since it fundamentally has no reason to destroy itself. Since gravity is a constant force the particle velocity is controlled by the particle size; the great mystery is how the graviton produces movement with 100% efficiency!

There are 4 fundamental forces that have been identified. In our present Universe they have rather different properties. The point is that Force equal's mass times (multiplied by) acceleration. In order for there to be a force the substance must have mass. Properties of the Fundamental Forces are as follows:

- The *strong interaction* is very strong, but very short-ranged. It acts only over ranges of order 10^{-13} centimeters and is responsible for holding the nuclei of atoms together. It is basically attractive, but can be effectively repulsive in some circumstances.

- The *electromagnetic force* causes electric and magnetic effects such as the repulsion between like electrical charges or the interaction of bar magnets. It is long-ranged, but much weaker than the strong force. It can be attractive or repulsive, and acts only between pieces of matter carrying electrical charge.

- The *weak force* is responsible for radioactive decay and neutrino interactions. It has a very short range and, as its name indicates, it is very weak.

- The *gravitational force* is weak, but very long ranged. Furthermore, it is always attractive, and acts between any two pieces of matter in the Universe since mass is its source. There is a rather strong belief (although it is yet to be confirmed experimentally) that in the very early Universe when temperatures were very high compared with today, the weak, electromagnetic, and strong forces were unified into a single force. Only when the temperature dropped did these forces separate from each other, with the strong force separating first and then at a still lower temperature the electromagnetic and weak forces separating to leave us with the 4 distinct forces that we see in our present Universe. The process of the forces separating from each other is called *spontaneous symmetry breaking*.

The major point here is that a force requires mass.

There is further speculation, which is even less firm than that above, that at even higher temperatures (the Planck Scale) all four forces were unified into a single force. Then, as the temperature dropped, gravitation separated first and then the other 3 forces separated as described above. The time and temperature scales for this proposed sequential loss of unification are illustrated in the following table.

Loss of Unity in the Forces of Nature			
Characterization	Forces Unified	Time Since Beginning	Temperature (GeV)*
All 4 forces unified	Gravity, Strong, Electromagnetic, Weak	~0	~infinite
Gravity separates (Planck Scale)	Strong, Electromagnetic, Weak	10-43 s	1019
Strong force separates (GUTs Scale)	Electromagnetic, Weak	10-35 s	1014
Split of weak and electromagnetic forces	None	10-11 s	100
Present Universe	None	1010 y	10-12

(Time and temperature scales for the proposed sequential loss of unification.)

Theories that postulate the unification of the strong, weak, and electromagnetic forces are called *Grand Unified Theories* (often known by the acronym GUTs). Theories that add gravity to the mix and try to unify all four fundamental forces into a single force are called *Superunified Theories*. The theory that describes the unified electromagnetic and weak interactions is called the *Standard Electroweak Theory*, or sometimes just the *Standard Model*.

Grand Unified and Superunified Theories remain theoretical speculations that are as yet unproven, but there is strong experimental evidence for the unification of the electromagnetic and weak interactions in the Standard

Electroweak Theory. Furthermore, although GUTs are not proven experimentally, there is strong circumstantial evidence to suggest that a theory at least like a Grand Unified Theory is required to make sense of the Universe. http://csep10.phys.utk.edu/astr162/lect/cosmology/forces.html

In order for all four forces to be unified into one force there would be two requirements. First the unified force must have mass or it would not be a force. The second would require the electron and the other particles associated with creating a force to break down into the one particle associated with all four forces. The evidence for this can be seen in the structure of light. Light can produce many different wavelengths with big differences in characteristics. The infrared wavelength of light produces heat and the ultraviolent wavelength produces bacteria killing and DNA damaging results.

The author disagrees with the above table, since Force equals mass times acceleration and at time zero there would be no unified force. There would be no force at all, since time is defined mathematically as Time = distance / velocity. At time zero nothing would be moving, since time is a measure of movement. Thus no mass and no movement would result in no unified force. Moreover, the main point is that in order for a unified force to occur, all the different particles that move and create a force would have to be unified in a specific wavelength and frequency similar to light. For nothing to form out of emptiness; then for nothing to produce something means everything is the same according to the big bang. If good and evil are the same, that would be the definition of incomprehensible.

The term infinite in the definition of an infinite universe does not imply that there is an infinite amount of "Something" in the Universe. The Infinite Universe requires that there is a certain absolute number of "Something" in the Universe that does not increase or decrease in number. Therefore, it is the perfect number based on the mathematical proofs that 1 does not equal 0. The author does not know the exact number of something that has mass and is the alpha and omega of all creation in the universe.

Numbers are a very important part of life and religion. In the Torah, there is a scroll called Numbers. The Mole, which is used by chemists to count atoms or molecules, can give us an idea of just how massive numbers can be. A sip of water or 18ml is equivalent to one mole or six hundred and two sextillion water molecules. If everyone on the planet started counting at one thousand water molecules per second, it would take over two thousand years to count the water in 18ml or a sip. What does "Something" look like; scripture states that only the pure in Heart will see God.

So, why does evil exist? Free will and without freewill, God would lack choice. Balance is the nature of perfection in the Infinite Universe. In an Infinite Universe the total amount of something remains constant. When an atom is divided it no longer has the characteristics of the original element, which displays the creative nature of "Something". Changing the number of protons in an element changes the physical appearance of the atom. This is truly remarkable, because an atom with one proton has a totally different appearance than an atom with 79 protons. Gold and hydrogen are very different, but extraordinarily similar. If Gold were the devil and hydrogen a saint, then Gold would constantly desire others to think it is more appealing or better than hydrogen. The devil does not care that God made him; he is too concerned about what others think. The devil displays a weakness and it would be a major lack of self-confidence. Jesus displayed incredible self-confidence and it upset the establishment. If you hear the truth and ignore it, then whom will you lead?

Furthermore, there is a point where matter can't be divided and at this final point of splitting or division "Something" and "Nothing" are distinctly defined. In the infinite Universe, the term infinite is used to describe the difference between something (1) and nothing (0). There is an infinite difference between zero and one.

According to Einstein, the universe is a space time continuum that can take one of three forms, determined by the amount of matter and energy it contains. A universe that is a continuum is an infinite universe. It is a universe that lacks a beginning and it will never end. This is the very definition of a continuum. Only substances that are finite can endings be predicted, thus when the universe is described as having a beginning we should hear next about its predictable ending. Things that are finite are predictable, such as the elements and radioactive decay or the human life span.

Can the universe change shape? Yes, according to Einstein's equation $E=MC^2$. The shape of the universe is determined by the amount of matter and energy it contains.

The possible shapes are as follows:

1. Positive curvature: The cosmos is like a sphere. Travel far enough and you'll come back to the starting point. Draw a triangle, and it will have more than 180 degrees. Without dark energy, this universe will slow, stop and recluse, with dark energy, the expansion will continue.

2. Flat: You'll never return to your starting point: triangles have precisely 180 degrees, as they do in geometry. Even without dark energy, this universe will expand forever, out more and more slowly all the time. With it, the expansion gets even faster. This is the shape of our universe according to the latest observations

3. Negative Curvature: Travelers never return: triangles always have less than 180 degrees. And expansion will barely slow, even without dark energy.

When the ratio of Matter to energy changes in the Universe, then the Universe can change Shape, based on $E=MC^2$ which states matter and energy are interchangeable. The universe is capable of changing its shape.

- Positive curvature: Ratio of Matter is much greater than energy

- Flat: Ratio of Matter to energy is about equal

- Negative Curvature: Ratio of Mater is much less than energy (More energy and less matter)

In a finite Universe something can increase in quantity, since nothing is used to produce more of something. This type of Universe is described to have begun many years ago everywhere at once. The Big Bang explains God in the Universe as everything. The intentions of the Big Bang Theory were good, but its very idea indicates that "Nothing" is the all-powerful God of the Universe. Finally, according to the Big Bang Theory, the all-powerful "Nothing" created "Something" out of emptiness. However, this gives "Nothing" power over "Something", since it is its creator. Our God is a jealous God, since He is greater than nothing! He is all powerful, the Alpha and Omega.

God is infinite in the Universe in him time has no beginning nor ending. Because God is infinite, he is the alpha and omega of all creation. "In God We Trust" is printed on United States currency. So what God does our government support? If it supports an incomprehensible God, then it will promote laws that say yes to behaviors that need a no. If a child yells loud enough, then the parent should not reward the child with what the child wants. The child will grow up lacking self-control and most likely end up in prison. A high prison population represents a government that is promoting an incomprehensible God, since most crime is not reported or goes unsolved.

Sin or the foundation of government make no sense when an incomprehensible God is promoted to the people with in God we trust. The goal of Science is to determine the truth. Currently the truth being taught in the public education system is only that of the Finite Universe resulting from the Big Bang. Religion seeks to control the mind of its followers, by providing no choice or freewill associated with decisions. The goal of the author is to promote the possibilities and allow the reader to make their own choice based on freewill.

The following link shows how new advancements in Chemistry are demonstrating how the basic building blocks of life can be assembled from nonliving elements: http:// www.pbs.org/wgbh/nova/evolution/where-did-we-come-from.html Moreover, the goal of science is to determine the truth.

Our universe is either finite or infinite. The reader has to make a choice. The Total Existence Theory compares the finite universe to the infinite universe and allows the reader to make a choice based on the educated conclusions presented. The choices we make determine our fate by revealing whether we believe the word became flesh making God capable of being understood. Love is defined by the choices we make based on beliefs. If we are not required to make a choice based on beliefs, then it would be impossible to show love.

Chapter 3

Chemistry

> Like an apple tree among the trees of the forest is
> my lover among the young men. I delight to sit in
> his shade, and his fruit is sweet to my taste.

Song of Songs

The Chemistry wasn't right, so the relationship ended. Is it odd that relationships can be tied to nonliving elements? There is even a match making website called Chemistry.com that singles can use to find the best mate. With this in mind, what does the average person need to know about chemistry to help them find the best mate and have a better relationship? Humans are made of nonliving atoms, so understanding their nature and why they are placed or grouped in families will provide the reader with a better understanding of the nonliving DNA molecules producing chemical behaviors in the human body. Both molecular compounds and ionic compounds form a bond based on balance. Sodium and chlorine ions form a bond based on balance (table salt—marriage), they will remain bonded until they are dissolved (table salt added to water). The point here is that a lot of events can lead to a marriage being dissolved.

The atom is composed of the proton, neutron, and electron. The proton and neutron are located in the nucleus and the electron moves outside the nucleus. The electron moves too fast to easily bond with the proton and form a neutron which keeps the atom stable. Electrons repel each other outside the nucleus, because they do not form a stable product when forced together, kind of like water and oil. It has been said, that DNA controls how you look. The DNA is getting a little too much credit. DNA only arranges the atoms in your body, it is not responsible for how the body looks, since white light allows some photons to be absorbed into white skin and many more into black skin. In a room with no light all humans are black, and a red shirt in a room with no light is black. This may seem unexpected, however it is the truth. The atoms in your hand are arranged in a mixture that reflects light to the eyes; the proton is the primary controller of looks. The proton is located in the nucleus of the atom and when its number increases or decreases, then the look of the atom changes. Silver and gold look different because of the proton. Moreover, all of the elements on the periodic table are made of three primary units, the proton, the neutron, and the electron. Helium has the atomic structure of Hydrogen within it. Lithium has the atomic structure of Helium and Hydrogen within it. The periodic table may seem complex; however each element builds on what already works. (Genesis 2:21-23) Eve has Adam's bone within her, just like Helium has the structure of Hydrogen in its electron cloud.

The Elements on the periodic table are classified biologically as non-living, so the purpose of comparing element behaviour to human behaviour or non-living behaviour to living behaviour concerns learning more about the elements; and their interaction within the periodic table. Human behaviour can change just like elements can change into other elements. The goal of this chapter concerns learning how to help humans be better communicators and friends with other groups of people that they would not normally be friends, since the second commandment is associated with loving our neighbour. Western culture compared to Eastern culture treat women very differently.

A culture that suppresses women still blames them for the fall of Adam and Eve. In Western culture, why does the man ask the woman to marry him? This is not a tradition found in the apes or a process that natural selection would support. Why should the woman have so much authority concerning whether the relationship should last? If a man forces a woman into a relationship, can he ever trust her? Will he ever know for sure that she loves him? John 12:43 shows that men desire praise from others. The family is where confidence starts. Love is defined by the choices we make, and a man will have no confidence without a purpose. The purpose of life concerns creating the eternal spirit. The character of the spirit is determined by the choices of the parents. (Genesis 16:12) A man desires a woman that is committed, one he can trust, so that his children do not become wild asses and leave his name worthy of shame. So, how does this correlate to the elements? Non-metals' will chose to bond with a metal based on the affinity series of the metals. Non-metals' determine whether reactions take place, since they are light and usually in the gas state and most of all have the desire for an electron.

Mendeleev was the first to receive credit for grouping the elements into families, so that their behaviour could be predicted. Elements in the same family have similar behaviours, just like people who are in the same family have similar behaviours. In the picture below, students have placed the elements in groups based on properties determined from experimentation.

(Dmitri Mendeleev formulated a periodic table similar to the one we use today. Elements were grouped by students according to recurring trends demonstrating Mendeleev's periodic table.)

Group 1, the alkali metal atoms contain a singles electron outside a noble—gas configuration, and so the valence electron is-well shielded from nuclear charge and the atomic radii are relatively large. The large volume of each atom results in a low density—small enough that Li, Na, and K float on water as they react with it. Li, Na, K, Rb, and Cs are all group IA elements, also known as the alkali metals. The seventh member of the group, francium (Fr) is radioactive and so rare that only 20 atoms of Fr may exist on Earth at any given moment. The term *alkali* is derived from an Arabic word meaning "ashes." Compounds of potassium as well as other alkali metals were obtained from wood ashes by early chemists. All the alkali metals are soft and, except for Cs which is yellow, are silvery-gray in color. Lithium, sodium, potassium, rubidium, and cesium have a great many other properties in common. All are solids at 0°C and melt below 200°C. Each has metallic properties such as good conduction of heat and electricity, malleability (the ability to be hammered into sheets), and ductility (the ability to be drawn into wires). The high thermal (heat) conductivity and the relatively low melting point (for a metal) of sodium make it an ideal heat-transfer fluid. It is used to cool certain types of nuclear reactors (liquid-metal fast breeder reactors, LMFBRs) and to cool the valves of high-powered automobile engines for this reason. If men are like metals, how would an alkali male behave? When alkali metals react with oxygen they form ashes, which mean they to not form gases. An ash is a solid ionic compound composed of the metal and nonmetal. Alkali men are good providers, since they desire to remain in a married state. Alkali metals display a very reactive state when in their elemental state; they are explosive in the presence of water. All the alkali metals are strong reducing agents. They are quite reactive, even reducing water. Hydrogen is in the alkali metal group; however it is not explosive in the presence of water.

The point here is that as the metals in the group grow in mass they have more strength associated with the properties of the group. Metallic bonding for the alkali metal can be compared to how well the alkali male forms male friendships. Weak attraction for the valence electron also results in weak metallic bonding, because it is attraction among nuclei and numerous valence electrons that holds metal atoms together. Weak metallic bonding results in low melting points, especially for the larger atoms toward the bottom of the group. Cs, for example, melts just above room temperature. Weak metallic bonding also accounts for the fact that all these metals are rather soft. For the alkali male it is not easy for him to form male friendships, because he is so strongly bonded to a female. The alkali male is a straight heterosexual.

Group 2, alkaline earth metals are all found in the Earth's crust, but not in the elemental form as they are so reactive. Instead, they are widely distributed in rock structures. They are alkaline metals, since they form bases in the presence of water. The main minerals in which magnesium is found are carnellite, magnesite and dolomite. Calcium is found in chalk, limestone, gypsum and anhydrite. Magnesium is the eighth most abundant element in the Earth's crust, and calcium is the fifth. The metals of Group 2 are harder and denser than sodium and potassium, and have higher melting points. These properties are due largely to the presence of two valence electrons on each atom, which leads to stronger metallic bonding than occurs in Group 1.

Of the elements in this Group only magnesium is produced on a large scale. It is extracted from sea-water by the addition of calcium hydroxide, which precipitates out the less soluble magnesium hydroxide. This hydroxide is then converted to the chloride, which is electrolyzed in a Downs cell to extract magnesium metal. Atomic and ionic radii increase smoothly down the Group. The ionic radii are all much smaller than the corresponding atomic radii. This is because the atom contains two electrons in an s level relatively far from the nucleus, and it is these electrons which are removed to form the ion. Remaining electrons are thus in levels closer to the nucleus, and in addition the increased effective nuclear charge attracts the electrons towards the nucleus and decreases the size of the ion.

Magnesium is the only Group 2 element used on a large scale. It is used in flares, tracer bullets and incendiary bombs as it burns with a brilliant white light. It is also alloyed with aluminum to produce a low-density, strong material used in aircraft. Magnesium oxide has such a high melting point it is used to line furnaces.

If men are like metals, then what characteristics would group two men possess? Group two men have excellent balance. They have a strong desire to be married and stay married. When metals bond together, they are called alloys; they are not considered compounds because an alloy does not have a consistent formula or pattern. Ferro Silicon Calcium / Calcium Silicide alloys are used for various purposes such as alloying element & a deoxidizer in different industrial applications. Calcium Aluminum Alloys act as the reducing agent for the smelting of rare metals. Moreover, group two men have excellent management skills, since they maintain strong male friendships in balance with their commitment to a spouse.

Groups 3-12 are known as the transition metals. There are a lot of men who fall into the transition metal group, since this type of metal changes its behavior relative to the non-metal in proximity. They are transition because they are capable of obtaining more than one overall charge, such as Fe^{2+}, and Fe^{3+}. The ten transition metal groups depend on nonmetals to determine their charge or behavior. Group 3 elements are generally hard metals with low aqueous solubility, and have low availability to the biosphere. No group 3 element has any documented biological role in living organisms. They are usually oxidized to the +3 oxidation state, even though scandium, yttrium and lanthanum can form lower oxidation states. The group 4 elements are not known to be involved in the biological chemistry of any living systems. They are hard refractory metals with low aqueous solubility and low availability to the biosphere. As tetravalent transition metals, all three elements form various inorganic compounds, generally in the oxidation state of +4. Group 5 contains vanadium (V), niobium (Nb), tantalum (Ta) anddubnium (Db). This group lies in the d-block of the periodic table. The group itself has not acquired a trivial name; it belongs to the broader grouping of the transition metals. Generally in the oxidation state of +5; lower oxidation states are also known, but they are less stable, decreasing in stability with atomic mass increase. Group 6 is notable in that it contains some of the only elements in periods 5 and 6 with a known role in the biological chemistry of living organisms: molybdenum is common in enzymes of many organisms, and tungsten has been identified in an analogous role in enzymes from some Achaea, such as *Pyrococcus furiosus*. The metals form compounds in different oxidation states: chromium forms compounds in all states from –2 to +6, but the stability of the +6 state grows down the group. Manganese is the only common Group 7 element. The most common oxidation states of manganese are +2, +3, +4, +6 and +7, though oxidation states from –3 to +7 are observed. Group 8 consists of iron (Fe), ruthenium (Ru), osmium (Os) and hassium (Hs). Iron exists in a wide range of oxidation states, –2 to +6, although +2 and +3 are the most common. Group 9 members are cobalt (Co), rhodium (Rh), iridium (Ir) and meitnerium (Mt). Cobalt is an essential trace nutrient to all animals, found in vitamin B-12. In its compounds cobalt nearly always exhibits a +2 or +3 oxidation state. Group 10 metals are white to light grey in color, and possess a high luster, a resistance to tarnish (oxidation) at STP, are highly ductile, and enter into oxidation states of +2 and +4, with +1 being seen in special conditions. The existence of a +3 state is debated, as the state could be an illusory state created by +2 and +4 states. Group 11 the "coinage metals" highlight the special physio-chemical properties that make this series of metals uniquely well suited for monetary purposes. These properties include ease of identification, resistance to tarnish, extreme difficulty in counterfeiting, durability, and a reliable store of value unmatched by any other metals known. Copper forms a rich variety of compounds with oxidation states +1 and +2, which are often called cuprous and cupric, respectively. Group 12 is also known as the volatile metals, although this can also more generally refer to any metal that has high volatility, such as polonium or flerovium. The three group 12 elements that occur naturally are zinc, cadmium and mercury. They are all widely used in electric and electronic applications, as well as in various alloys. Mercury exists in two main oxidation states, I and II. Higher oxidation states are unimportant, but have been detected, e.g., mercury (IV) fluoride (HgF4) but only under extraordinary conditions.

The main group metals are separated in the periodic table by the transition metals. When men behave like transition metals, they spend more or less money depending on the attractively of the female. This is part of the reason women spend time putting on makeup before a date. The financial role of the male will be that of the provider, since he is most similar to the metal in that he loses his reproductive genetic information and the metal loses its electron to become stable.

The general trend down Group 13 is from non-metallic to metallic character. Boron is a non-metal with a covalent network structure. The other elements are considerably larger than boron and consequently are more ionic and metallic in character. Aluminum has a close-packed metallic structure but is on the borderline between ionic and covalent character in its compounds. The remainder of Group 13 are generally considered to be metals, although some compounds exhibit covalent characteristics. These elements are not found free in nature, but are all present in various minerals and ores. The most important aluminium-containing minerals are bauxite and cryolite. Aluminium is the most widely used element in this Group. It is obtained by the electrolysis of aluminium oxide, which is purified from bauxite. The melting point of the aluminium oxide is too high for electrolysis of the melt, so instead it is dissolved in molten cryolite. The expected similarity in appearance between elements in the same Group is much less apparent in Group 14, where there is a considerable change in character on descending the Group. Carbon is a dull black color in the form of graphite, or hard and transparent in the form of diamond; silicon and germanium are dull grey or black; tin and lead are a shiny grey color.

In Group 14 the elements change from non-metallic in character at the top of the Group to metallic at the bottom. Carbon is a non-metal, silicon and germanium are metalloids, and tin and lead are typical metals. The general reactivity of the Group as a whole is therefore difficult to ascertain, and the reactivity of each element must be considered individually. Carbon exists in two important allotropic forms, diamond and graphite. Diamond has an extended covalently-bonded structure in which each carbon atom is bonded to four others. This compact, rigid arrangement explains why diamond is both extremely hard and chemically inert. Graphite has a layer structure. Planes of covalently-bonded carbon atoms are held together by weak van der Waals forces, and slide over each other easily. Chemically, graphite is more reactive than diamond but still does not react easily. However, it does oxidize at high temperatures and this is the reason why carbon is used in various forms as fuel. Silicon is chemically unreactive. Germanium is also unreactive and not widely used, so will not be considered further. It does, however, have excellent semi-conducting properties so may become more widely used in a few years' time. Both tin and lead are generally unreactive metals. Tin has two common allotropes. At room temperature the stable form is white tin; below 286.2K the stable form is grey tin. Tin has a tendency to displace lead, and not vice versa as may be expected. In general, chemical reactivity increases on descending the Group.

The appearance of the Group 15 elements varies widely. Nitrogen is a colorless, odorless gas; phosphorus exists in white, red and black solid forms; arsenic is found in yellow and grey solid forms; antimony is found in a metallic or amorphous grey form; and finally bismuth is a white, crystalline, brittle metal. These appearances reflect the changing nature of the elements as the Group is descended, from non-metal to metal. The elements of Group 15 show a marked trend towards metallic character on descending the Group. This trend is reflected both in their structures and in their chemical properties, as for example in the oxides which become increasingly basic.

The first element of Group 16, oxygen, is the only gas, and is colorless and odorless. Sulfur is a pale yellow, brittle solid. Selenium can have either an amorphous or a crystalline structure; the amorphous form can be red or black, and the crystalline form can be red or grey. Tellurium is a silvery-white color with a metallic luster. Polonium is a naturally radioactive element. Oxygen and sulfur are highly electronegative elements—the electronegativity of oxygen is second only to that of fluorine. Their general reactivity is therefore dominated by their ability to gain electrons. There is a transition down the Group from non-metallic to more metallic properties, so that oxygen is a non-metal and tellurium a metalloid. All the elements except polonium form M^{2-} ions. There is a marked difference between oxygen and the other members of the Group. This arises from (a) the small size of the O atom which enables it to form double bonds (b) its inability to expand its valence shell like the other elements as it has no accessible d-orbitals (c) its high electronegativity, which enables it to participate in hydrogen-bonding.

The elements of Group 17, the Halogens, are a very similar set of non-metals. They all exist as diatomic molecules, X2, and oxidise metals to form halides. The halogen oxides are acidic, and the hydrides are covalent. Fluorine is the most electronegative element of all. Generally, electronegativity and oxidising ability decrease on descending the Group. The result of this decreasing electronegativity is increased covalent character in the compounds, so that AlF3 is ionic whereas AlCl3 is covalent. Fluorine shows some anomalies because of the small size of its atom and ion. This allows several F atoms to pack around a different central atom, as in $AlF6^{3-}$ compared with $AlCl4^{-}$. The F-F bond is also unexpectedly weak because the small size of the F atom brings the lone pairs closer together than in other halogens, and repulsion weakens the bond. The halogens are too reactive to occur free in nature. Fluorine is mined as fluorspar, calcium fluoride and cryolite. It is extracted by electrolysis as no oxidant will oxidise fluorides to fluorine. Chlorine is also found in minerals such as rock-salt, and huge quantities of chloride ions occur in seawater, inland lakes and subterranean brine wells. It is obtained by the electrolysis of molten sodium chloride or brine.

Group 18, the noble gases are all found in minute quantities in the atmosphere, and are isolated by fractional distillation of liquid air. Helium can be obtained from natural gas wells where it has accumulated as a result of radioactive decay. The noble gases do have certain important industrial functions: Helium is used by divers to dilute the oxygen they breathe, Argon is widely used to provide an inert atmosphere for high-temperature metallurgical processes; Neon and argon are used for filling discharge tubes. Based on the periodic table metals have more different groups than nonmetals. Specifically the transition metals have multiple behaviors, since those metals can gain and lose electrons in multiple amounts. The apple does not fall far from the tree, thus men display more complicated behaviors than women. Women are more predictable, since some desire more like control Fluorine, while others like Iodine need only a little.

The periodic table is not an Astrology tool meant to determine your fate like the moon or stars. The goal is for the reader to understand that Men like to trade and women like to share. Compromise is required for the relationship to be successful. Also, just like the metals and nonmetals will react if not stored properly. Cheating or an affair happens because the man or woman thought they could stop the reaction before liftoff.

Once the steps are in sequence and the elements are close enough, then a reaction will occur. Buildings can burn down, if chemicals are not stored properly. Remind yourself of who you love daily, because the mind is forgetful. Focus on the things those you love do correctly as a means to prevent an affair. Chemicals have to be stored correctly or they will react.

Those that have an affair are likely to have multiple affairs, and that increases the chance over time to get a sexually transmitted disease. The disease could be bacterial or viral and produce toxins that lead to cancer. Cancer cells are anaerobic which means they survive without the presence of oxygen. The purpose of the cancer cell is to isolate the toxin and prevent it from spreading to other organs. Often cancer cells will disappear when the toxin is removed from the body. Chemicals that are tested and shown to cause cancer in the lab are labeled as carcinogenic. Sweetpoison, written by author Dr. Janet Starr Hull, is a book exposing aspartame dangers found commonly in diet drinks and chewing gum labeled as Phenylalanine. SweetPoison.com provides a variety of aspartame information including nutritional advice on aspartame detoxification, aspartame side effects and up-to-date information on aspartame dangers. Some toxins are more easily removed than others, once a sexually transmitted disease takes hold it gets in multiple cells and becomes complex to remove based on each person's DNA.

It is difficult to not describe the elements as living, since they undergo radioactive decay or have a birth and death and appear finite. Also, the isotope abundance for each element is in balance which provides a consistent means to measure mass and determine concentration. The elements combine and form DNA, the genetic information that controls the cell is responsible for reproduction and it controls the life and death of the cell. When a cell becomes cancerous it does not know how to die. Cancer is considered to be uncontrolled cell growth. In the nucleus of the atom, the neutron works in a similar way. The neutron under a process called radioactive decay, splits into a proton and electron. This process makes elements finite, which means that elements have a birth and death. When the body dies and it is buried, the carbon undergoes radioactive decay. Thus in 5000 yrs only half of the body will remain if it was unearthed, unless the body was near colder temperatures. Temperature is a measure of motion, so less movement could prevent fewer neutrons from being split. The main point is that the neutron controls the birth and death of the element. An exception to this would be Fusion, which occurs under high pressure and high heat in places like our Sun.

Radioactive decay of Carbon is an important concept to understand, since it is the basis for theories about the origin of life. When scientists say that life most likely did not originated from outer space, it is because travel time would cause the DNA to become destroyed due to the radioactive decay of carbon. Most scientists think life originated on Earth because of the radioactive decay of carbon. Furthermore, we have yet to discover life and prove it is living on any other planet or other place.

What is Chemistry the study of? Matter... Yes, however most of the effort is spent examining the electron. The electron controls the behavior of the element. It is found on the outside of the nucleus and it is a form of energy, so it moves in waves around the nucleus. The electron does not move like a Planet around the Sun in a direct path. The electron is the largest particle considered to be energy; its mass is measurable although it is not used for calculating the mass of the element. It is like the hair on your body, when you get a haircut it does not affect your overall weight. However, just because the electron has a small mass does not mean it is insignificant. The behavior of the element is a huge issue. The periodic table is organized based on the behavior of the elements. The shape of periodic table is the result of the electron. When bleach is poured on cloths, it is the electron that caused the color change. When we go to the doctor and ask for medicine that will help cure a specific behavior, then we are asking for a remedy that will target an electron change. How the elements stick together is based on the electron, so learning how to control and manipulate that behavior results in new products.

The proton desires the reader to remember that it is responsible for your physical looks. The neutron desires the reader to remember that it is responsible for your eventual return to dust, since carbon decays into Nitrogen. Nitrogen is a gas and makes up 80% of our atmosphere. So those who were buried, which prevented them from being eaten by other organisms will undergo radioactive decay. Specifically, carbon decay since we are carbon based life. Lastly, the electron desires the reader to remember that it is responsible for your innate physical behavior. If you are normal or have any type of chemical imbalance, then thank the electron.

So, what does this have to do with relationships? Metals are found on the left side of the periodic table, because these elements tend to lose electrons so that they become more stable. Sodium in its metal state is very unstable, if it is placed in water it will explode. Thus metals, like men desire to lose their electrons. Most men constantly think about reproduction, which concerns the joining of the sperm with the egg. Just like the elements, there are different degrees of loss. Calcium is not as reactive as Sodium and gold even though it is not a noble gas, it behaves like a good priest.

Nonmetals are found on the right side of the periodic table and they harbor a lot of power. All chemical reactions take place because of the nonmetals. The above picture demonstrates compound formation. There are two primary groups of compounds the ionic and molecular. The molecular contain nonmetals only and the ionic contain both metals and nonmetals. Male only friendships are similar to Metallic bonds, because men like to trade just about anything. The image below demonstrates how metals will bond with nonmentals to form a compound. The important point to note is that there is a balance associated with the giver and the receiver.

(Ions are created when an atom either gains or losses electrons. Students demonstrate comprehension of this with the formation of compounds resulting from grouping ions together that produce an overall charge of zero or balanced.)

Female only friendships are similar to covalent bonds, since women like to share. Male and Female relationships are similar to ionic bonds, since both get balance from the loss (metals lose electrons to become stable like noble gases) and gain (nonmetals gain electrons to become stable like noble gases). Nonmetals have the desire for the electron and Fluorine has the greatest. In a stream of Fluorine gas wood and rubber will burst into flames. So where does this apply in the relationship world?

Why do affairs happen? Sometimes, the stronger nonmetal desires to be with the metal that is a better provider. In a pool of elements like, Sodium, Calcium, Oxygen, and Chlorine, the sodium and chlorine are going to produce the compound sodium chloride. Once you have chosen your significant other, then you need to protect yourself. Don't put yourself in a situation that is going to cause you to have an affair. Once an illusion starts about the possibilities of a new relationship, then an affair is likely just like Fluorine will make the move to Sodium without hesitation. Chemicals are stored in a laboratory based on a safety code.

When metals come in contact with nonmetals, the metals transfer their electrons to the nonmetals'. Sounds kind of romantic in a novel kind of way... A transfer is a give and take; however the nonmetal is the one that holds on to the electron. Thus in a relationship the female is the one that typically holds on to the words exchanged. A male can get upset when a woman does not listen to him. In the church, men trade tasks making males Elders and Deacons and women responsible for the children. Some churches share these responsibilities, however if all tasks are shared then Men will lose interest. A trade is risky; just ask those who lost money invested in stock during the recent financial bank failures. A woman will hold on to the word of a man that she cares about! Metals can also bind with themselves to form what is called an alloy. Steel is an example; it has the element iron and Molybdenum, Magnesium and Chromium. Metals work together to form what is termed a metallic bond and when more than one metal bond they form an alloy as shown in the penny lab below. The penny is treated with sodium hydroxide and Zinc then heated to from brass.

(One of the supreme quests of a alchemy is to transmute lead into gold. Lead atomic number 82 and gold atomic number 79 are defined as elements by the number of protons they possess. Students learn of Alchemy with a demonstration about the formation of the alloy brass.)

In this bond, Metals trade electrons with each other. Steel is magnetic, since the electrons are not traded at the same rate and that sets up two parts of a magnet, an area of electron gain or negative part of the magnet and electron loss or positive part of the magnet. When nonmetals come in contact with nonmetals' they form what is called a covalent bond. In a covalent bond, electrons are shared between the nonmetals.

The point here is that there is a drastic difference between a share and a trade. Men have an innate desire to trade. Boys trade baseball cards, they trade silly bands; as they grow into men they trade stocks in the stock market. A trade is risky. Men desire to trade. Around the house, men think lets trade tasks. The man will mow the lawn and he thinks the woman should do the laundry. When the man comes in from mowing the lawn, he does not want to do help put away laundry. Why? Man thinks trade, he does this task and she does that task. The image below illustrates the balance associated with producing new compounds or with decomposition the production of elements. The process is predictable based on the law of conservation of mass.

(The law of conservation of mass, or principle of mass conservation, states that for any system closed to all transfers of matter and energy, the mass must remain constant over time. Students demonstrate an understanding of this principle by balancing the number of compounds or elements in the reactants with those produced in the products.)

Women desire to share. Girls share dolls, cloths, and as they grow up they desire to share responsibilities' with their future mate. A man that is sharing in every task around the house will eventually feel trapped and look for a way out. He will get involved with extra activities at work and this will prevent him from being around very often. A woman will begin to feel controlled, if she is not given the opportunity to share with her mate. The point here is that a balance needs to be met. The couple needs to decide which tasks around the home need to be shared and which need to be traded. This will be easy for some and very hard for others. Some men are just obsessive about trading, since it is at the heart of being a man in appearance. Balance in the relationship will prevent the waste associated with the divorcee or break up.

In a relationship, is balance important? Who should do what task? Since more women are now going to college, balancing the check book becomes a mutual task. The person who earns more usually determines how the money is spent. Colossians 3:18 states that a wife should submit herself to her husband; moreover the woman is usually the one that is in control of the relationship. She is the one that is traditionally asked to be married, and it is her decision to say yes or no. When she says no, she is in control of the submission process. If more men understood this, then there would be fewer in prison for stalking and rape. When she says yes, she is in control of the submission process. What can a man do to gain some control over this process? What should a man look for in a woman, if he wants her to submit to him? My wife and I hardly ever argue, because I view her as being smarter than me and I desire to be treated with the same respect. In an emergency, I desire my wife to have the confidence to make the best call and not be indecisive. If there is an issue, then I communicate the problem and possible solution and she gives her input and a decision is made.

Women do not like to be constantly told what to do, this is the point. Look for a woman with high educational and moral standards. Did you listen to what she had to say, since a woman seeks to constantly receive information from her lover? Weren't paying attention, how do you expect her to desire to submit? How we act or behave to others is usually how we are treated. Most men think that if they earn a lot of money, then the woman will submit to him. A man may think that a woman of interest is high maintenance and he can afford her, so she will submit to him when she sees his net worth. This is an illusion, since money can't control desire; affairs usually occur without the other knowing. If Bathsheba would not have gotten pregnant by King David, then nobody would have known of the affair. In Jewish tradition when something bad happens to you, then you must have done something wrong. (John 9:2)

Chapter 4

White Light

Nature and Nature's laws lay hid in night: God said, "Let Newton be!" and all was light.

Alexander Pope

What is the wavelength of white light, and is white light a mixture of the colors of the visible spectrum? White light is currently defined as a mixture of colors, and the photon a particle of light is currently defined as having zero mass. The purpose of this chapter is to challenge those theories by presenting new ideas.

Light is defined as a mixture of colors because it can be physically separated with a prism; however it behaves more like an allotrope that can be physically separated. Therefore white light should be defined as an allotrope that can be physically separated. The mass of white light can be theoretically calculated, however it has yet to be experimentally calculated because the particle is too small for our most advanced balance to measure and compare to the theoretical. Matter is classified into three common groups: Elements, Compounds, and Mixtures. The allotrope group is the area where nanotechnology holds the greatest promise for new products.

- Mixture—can be physically separated; these are the two types:

- Homogeneous mixture—coffee and water (has the same uniform appearance and composition throughout.)

- Heterogeneous mixture—Sand and salt (consists of visibly different substances or phases)

- Compound—a pure chemical substance consisting of two or more different chemical elements that can be separated into simpler substances by chemical reactions.

- Element—a pure chemical substance consisting of one type of atom distinguished by its atomic number, which is the number of protons.

- Allotropes—one of two or more different molecular forms of a substance in the same physical state. Oxygen (O_2) and Ozone (O_3) are examples

Red light has a specific frequency of photons compared to the frequency of Green light. When these two are put together they form yellow light which does not fit the definition of a physical mixture, since the yellow light is physically different in appearance from the green and red light, yet it is composed of only one substance called the photon. A mixture requires more than one substance, like a photon and a proton would be a mixture. Thus light behaves more like an allotrope than a mixture. It should be described as an allotrope that can be physically separated. Green and red light are both made of photons, so classifying light as a mixture is incorrect. Mixtures are made of two or more substances that don't have the same chemical structure or formula.

Is white light a mixture of the colors of the visible spectrum? A better explanation would be that White light has the energy to make all the colors of the spectrum. When we examine yellow light we don't see green or red light. White light has the ability to hold the photons necessary to make all the colors while keeping its specific wavelength as a guess.

Based on the following research, evidence indicates that white light has a wavelength distinctly different from the photons on the electromagnetic spectrum. Electrons move in waves and the alternating current allows them to be transported from one place to another. So energy can be described outside of the electromagnetic spectrum, since this spectrum only defines the frequency of the photon and not the electron. Energy is defined as anything that is an electron or smaller and moves in wave form. The electromagnetic spectrum provides a description of light based on consistent behavior. For example, equal proportions of green light and red light produce a yellow light. The yellow light has a specific wavelength 597-577nm. Yellow light does not have the wavelength from green to red 492-780nm, as it should base on the current definition of white light. This inconsistency indicates that something else is occurring.

When elements are burned electrons are pushed from one energy level to another. Where do the photons originate to produce the colors of light associated with the element being burned Energy is being forced into the element in the form of heat when the element is burned and that energy is stored in pockets. Each element has a certain set of pockets that allow the element to release the photons when the electron returns to its normal state. Burning the element is not a nuclear change. The stored photons in pockets within the electron cloud regroup based on the number of photons available which results in the frequency associated with the color displayed by the element being burned. Thus photons must have mass, since elements display different colors when burned. The number of photons determines the color of the frequency of light as illustrated in the picture below.

When an electron drops from a higher energy orbit to a lower energy orbit, photons are emitted in a specific frequency. Brandon demonstrates a chemical reaction that produces heat because of an electron transition to the 3rd energy level. The flame test demonstrates an electron transition to the 2nd.

(Atomic electron transition is a change of an electron from one quantum state to another within an atom. The farther the electron jumps, the shorter the wavelength of the photon emitted. Students demonstrate an electron transition with the burning of copper and its release of photons producing visible bluish-green color.)

The tables below on the density of water shows how solid and liquid behave and look distinctly different even though both are water.

The photon is undergoing a volume change, thus a density change throughout the collection of particles; similar to what is seen in liquid water and solid water. Thus a density change would result in the photons behaving differently or more condensed than the photons in the standard electromagnetic spectrum. When we examine the density of water, we see that water has a large number of density changes as the temperature changes.

The table below shows the densities of water. Whole degrees are listed down the left hand side of the table, while tenths of a degree are listed across the top.

So to find the density of water at say 5.4 °C, you would first find the whole degree by searching down the left hand column until you reach '5'. Then you would slide across that row until you reach the column labeled '0.4'. The density of water at 5.4 °C is 0.999957 g/mL.

	0.0	0.1	0.2	0.3	0.4	0.5	0.6	0.7	0.8	0.9
0	0.999841	0.999847	0.999854	0.999860	0.999866	0.999872	0.999878	0.999884	0.999889	0.999895
1	0.999900	0.999905	0.999909	0.999914	0.999918	0.999923	0.999927	0.999930	0.999934	0.999938
2	0.999941	0.999944	0.999947	0.999950	0.999953	0.999955	0.999958	0.999960	0.999962	0.999964
3	0.999965	0.999967	0.999968	0.999969	0.999970	0.999971	0.999972	0.999972	0.999973	0.999973
4	0.999973	0.999973	0.999973	0.999972	0.999972	0.999972	0.999970	0.999969	0.999968	0.999966
5	0.999965	0.999963	0.999961	0.999959	0.999957	0.999955	0.999952	0.999950	0.999947	0.999944
6	0.999941	0.999938	0.999935	0.999931	0.999927	0.999924	0.999920	0.999916	0.999911	0.999907
7	0.999902	0.999898	0.999893	0.999888	0.999883	0.999877	0.999872	0.999866	0.999861	0.999855
8	0.999849	0.999843	0.999837	0.999830	0.999824	0.999817	0.999810	0.999803	0.999796	0.999789
9	0.999781	0.999774	0.999766	0.999758	0.999751	0.999742	0.999734	0.999726	0.999717	0.999709
10	0.999700	0.999691	0.999682	0.999673	0.999664	0.999654	0.999645	0.999635	0.999625	0.999615
11	0.999605	0.999595	0.999585	0.999574	0.999564	0.999553	0.999542	0.999531	0.999520	0.999509
12	0.999498	0.999486	0.999475	0.999463	0.999451	0.999439	0.999427	0.999415	0.999402	0.999390
13	0.999377	0.999364	0.999352	0.999339	0.999326	0.999312	0.999299	0.999285	0.999272	0.999258
14	0.999244	0.999230	0.999216	0.999202	0.999188	0.999173	0.999159	0.999144	0.999129	0.999114
15	0.999099	0.999084	0.999069	0.999054	0.999038	0.999023	0.999007	0.998991	0.998975	0.998959
16	0.998943	0.998926	0.998910	0.998893	0.998877	0.998860	0.998843	0.998826	0.998809	0.998792
17	0.998774	0.998757	0.998739	0.998722	0.998704	0.998686	0.998668	0.998650	0.998632	0.998613
18	0.998595	0.998576	0.998558	0.998539	0.998520	0.998501	0.998482	0.998463	0.998444	0.998424
19	0.998405	0.998385	0.998365	0.998345	0.998325	0.998305	0.998285	0.998265	0.998244	0.998224
20	0.998203	0.998183	0.998162	0.998141	0.998120	0.998099	0.998078	0.998056	0.998035	0.998013
21	0.997992	0.997970	0.997948	0.997926	0.997904	0.997882	0.997860	0.997837	0.997815	0.997792
22	0.997770	0.997747	0.997724	0.997701	0.997678	0.997655	0.997632	0.997608	0.997585	0.997561
23	0.997538	0.997514	0.997490	0.997466	0.997442	0.997418	0.997394	0.997369	0.997345	0.997320
24	0.997296	0.997271	0.997246	0.997221	0.997196	0.997171	0.997146	0.997120	0.997095	0.997069
25	0.997044	0.997018	0.996992	0.996967	0.996941	0.996914	0.996888	0.996862	0.996836	0.996809
26	0.996783	0.996756	0.996729	0.996703	0.996676	0.996649	0.996621	0.996594	0.996567	0.996540
27	0.996512	0.996485	0.996457	0.996429	0.996401	0.996373	0.996345	0.996317	0.996289	0.996261
28	0.996232	0.996204	0.996175	0.996147	0.996118	0.996089	0.996060	0.996031	0.996002	0.995973
29	0.995944	0.995914	0.995885	0.995855	0.995826	0.995796	0.995766	0.995736	0.995706	0.995676
30	0.995646	0.995616	0.995586	0.995555	0.995525	0.995494	0.995464	0.995433	0.995402	0.995371

*(The density of water is relatively simple with the formula
Density=Mass/Volume. The author proposes that the photon has mass
and that a density change occurs to produce white light.)*

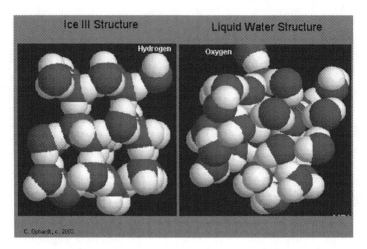

(Temperature is a measure of movement and the temperature change causes the molecule to alter its volume or space where it can move its mass.)

Also, a large change is observed at the boiling point even though the density of water gradually changes from freezing to boiling. Moreover, evidence indicates that white light has its own spectrum similar to the wavelengths that electrons occupy in an alternating current. White light has its own spectrum, because the photons grouped in white light are not behaving the same as a group of red light. Photons in white light must be experiencing a volume change. This would attribute to the lack of a specific wavelength for white light and challenge the current definition of white light as a mixture of all the colors. Since white light has its own spectrum, it can best be compared to the other colors based on its energy value.

Does the photon have mass? After all, it has energy and energy is equivalent to mass.

Quantum mechanics introduces the idea that light can be viewed as a collection of "particles"—photons. Even though these photons cannot be brought to rest, and so the idea of rest mass doesn't really apply to them.

If we now return to the question "Does light have mass?" this can be taken to mean different things if the light is moving freely or trapped in a container. The definition of the invariant mass of an object is m = sqrt{$E^2/c^4 - p^2/c^2$}. By this definition a beam of light is mass less like the photons it is composed of. However, if light is trapped in a box with perfect mirrors so the photons are continually reflected back and forth in both directions symmetrically in the box, then the total momentum is zero in the box's frame of reference but the energy is not. Therefore the light adds a small contribution to the mass of the box. This could be measured—in principle at least—either by the greater force required to accelerate the box, or by an increase in its gravitational pull. You might say that the light in the box has mass, but it would be more correct to say that the light contributes to the total mass of the box of light. You should not use this to justify the statement that light has mass in general (.http://math.ucr.edu/home/baez/physics/Relativity/SR /light_mass.html).

Relativistic mass is a measure of the energy E of a particle, which changes with velocity. By convention, relativistic mass is not usually called the mass of a particle in contemporary physics so, at least semantically, it is wrong to say the photon has mass in this way. But you can say that the photon has relativistic mass if you really want to. In modern terminology the mass of an object is its invariant mass, which is zero for a photon, because photons cannot be brought to rest. (http://math.ucr.edu/home/baez/physics/Relativit y/SR /light_mass.html).

Can the mass of light be calculated?

Yes, it can be mathematically calculated. The electron has a mass of 9.11 x 10^{-28} and 5.1 x 10^{14} photons can produce the photo-electric effect, then the mass of a photon can be calculated to be 1.8 x 10^{-42} g.

No, it can't be experimentally calculated. Trying to get a photon to rest on a balance is the problem. The Heisenberg Uncertainty principle states that it can't, since whenever something is measured it is changed. Thus the conclusion is that light has two properties. It has a wave property that is separate from its particle property. It does two things at once. Therefore this definition means the particle is not a characteristic of the wave and the wave is not a characteristic of the particle.

The case of photons and other particles that move at the speed of light is special. From the formula relating relativistic mass to invariant mass, it follows that the invariant mass of a photon must be zero, but its relativistic mass need not be. The phrase "The rest mass of a photon is zero" might sound nonsensical because the photon can never be at rest; but this is just a side effect of the terminology, since by making this statement, we can bring photons into the same mathematical formalism as the everyday particles that do have rest mass. In modern physics texts, the term mass when unqualified means invariant mass in most cases, and photons are said to be "mass less" http://math.ucr. edu/home/baez/physics/Relativity/SR/mass.html

If a light is placed in a room and turned on, then photons are being emitted from a source and are moving about the room. If the light is turned off, the photons are absorbed by the surroundings and stopped moving in the same sequence they were delivered. In space there is less matter to slow or absorb the photons, but eventually they will run into something and be absorbed. Light works like a train, instead of the train going in a straight line it moves in a wave. Why? It is easier for the train to stay connected when it moves in a wave. If a train moved in a straight path for many miles it would be easier for the train to break. The wave nature of light makes it flexible and even bendable. It would be expected that the photon is constantly modifying its density in order to produce the wave effect in the many different types of radiation on the electromagnetic spectrum. Like water and ice, an imbalance produces instability and modulation. Photons can and do come to rest all the time, by getting absorbed or stored in matter they strike. The point of getting a photon to rest when calculating its mass concerns understanding how mass is calculated. Mass is calculated on a balance, so that the force of gravity cancels out. Mass is calculated on a balance and weight is calculated on a scale. Less light is absorbed in space because of the low amount of matter present.

How does an atom produce various frequencies of photons? The flame test experiment provides clues to the synthesis. The approximate mass of a photon is 1.8×10^{-42} g, then how does an atom produce colors other than yellow? When a metal is burned this is a combustion reaction, which is a reaction in which the metal is combined with oxygen. Only electrons in transition from higher to lower levels lose energy and emit light. This is how light is produced; atoms produce light in this way in various reactions from nuclear to decomposition reactions. In the combustion reaction with Hydrogen and Oxygen, Oxygen is the source of light emitted. In the sun, a tremendous amount of input is required for a fusion reaction. Thus based on Newton's third law, the emitted light occurs when the fused atom goes from an excited state to ground state.

What about lightning? Lightning does not result from a chemical reaction or from a nuclear reaction. Lightning or the flow of electrons produces light. So how do only electrons produce light? Shouldn't lightning be expected to be yellow in color? However, white light denies what is expected since it is not considered a color and has a wavelength associated with all the colors. It is amazing how different metals when burned produce different colors. The volume available must be impacted by the density of the atom. Lightning moves so fast that it breaks the sound barrier, thus this type of movement must produce an environment similar to a vortex. The electrons are being drawn in to become a bolt of lightning. If we were to go back in time 3000 years, then we would see not light bulbs. Fire, lightning, and Stars were the primary sources of light at that time. Light is not continuously produced from a reaction, because the reactants are limited in the space where it is being produced. Stars stop producing light for several reasons. The volume available to the substance to store photons determines the frequency of light emitted. Is white a color, most would say it is not. White light is the densest way to transport photons from the Sun to the Earth for the purpose of photosynthesis, animal vision, and many others. White light is a miracle in a sense, because it denies what is expected.

So how does lighting produce light? Electrons can store photons without them changing the nature of the electron particle. This is huge, since particles are defined by their mass. Change the mass of the Neutron and it is no longer a Neutron. Electrons work as a team, the photons are like leafs on a roof of an electron when the wind moves the electrons together the photons attract to each other due to their own force of gravity. Once the electrons loose the excess photons the light from the lighting stops. Electrons produce light by working as a team. This occurs in the atom as well. An atom that is in an excited state has electrons in excited states. They work together to emit light at different frequencies depending on the number of photons available to the atom during an orbital transition. The photons are pushed from the atom by an excitement and pulled together by gravity to form a frequency that defines the element.

Why can the mass of light be mathematically calculated? According to Newton: For every action there is an equal and opposite reaction. The statement means that in every interaction, there is a pair of forces acting on the two interacting objects. The size of the forces on the first object equals the size of the force on the second object. F=MA (Force equals mass times acceleration) Thus, the mass of the photon can be calculated.

The mass of an electron is mathematically approximated to be 9.10×10^{-31} kg [1].

To move an electron it will take at least the mass of an electron to move it from one place to another based on Newton's third law. So, when enough sunlight (energy) is absorbed by the material (a semiconductor), electrons are dislodged from the material's atoms. These electrons do not move on their own, they must be pushed. Thus Newton's third law comes into play. This is significant, because it shows that the wave could be proven to be a characteristic of the particle.

Sunlight is composed of photons, or particles of solar energy. These photons contain various amounts of energy corresponding to the different wavelengths of the solar spectrum. When photons strike a photovoltaic cell, they may be reflected, pass right through, or be absorbed. Only the absorbed photons provide energy to generate electricity. When enough sunlight (energy) is absorbed by the material (a semiconductor), electrons are dislodged from the material's atoms. Special treatment of the material surface during manufacturing makes the front surface of the cell more receptive to free electrons, so the electrons naturally migrate to the surface.

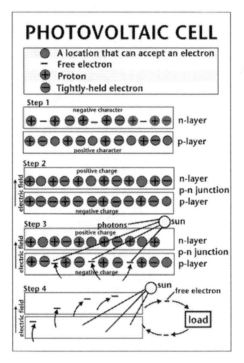

(A solar cell called a photovoltaic cell is an electrical device that converts the energy of light directly into electricity by the photovoltaic effect. The main point here is that in order for an object to move another object that is larger than it, the smaller object must be tightly woven together (dense) and act as a force capable of moving the larger object.)

When the electrons leave their position, holes are formed. When many electrons, each carrying a negative charge, travel toward the front surface of the cell, the resulting imbalance of charge between the cell's front and back surfaces creates a voltage potential like the negative and positive terminals of a battery. When the two surfaces are connected through an external load, electricity flows. http://w w w.solcomhouse.com/solarpower.htm

In the photoelectric effect, metals eject electrons called photoelectrons when light shines on them. The alkali metals Li, Na, K, Rb, and Cs are particularly subject to the effect. Not just any frequency of light will cause the photoelectric effect. Red light, for example, will not cause the ejection of photoelectrons from potassium, no matter how intense the light. Yet even a very weak yellow light ($v = 5.1 \times 10^{14} \, s^{-1}$) shining on potassium begins the effect.

The red frequency has a lower number of photons per second which explains why it can't push a photoelectron out of the alkali metal. The photons travel in sequence one after the other just like cars on a highway or bicyclists in a race. This explains why increasing the frequency causes the electrons to travel faster out of the alkali metal.

The weakest frequency provides the starting point in determination of an approximate mass of a photon. If 5.1×10^{14} photons per sec are shot at an alkali metal and it begins to release electrons, then it will be assumed to release one electron per 5.1×10^{14} photons per sec. Increasing the threshold frequency produces an increase in the number of electrons ejected, because the increasing the threshold frequency represents an increase in the light intensity. The starting point is important, since it provides a reference point. Increasing the frequency causes the electron to move faster which reinforces Newton's third law.

The following is the calculation for the relativistic mass of a Photon:

If it takes 5.1×10^{14} photons to emit one photoelectron, then an electron can be divided up into 5.1×10^{14} photons.

1 electron = 5.1×10^{14} photons

If the electron has a mass of 9.11×10^{-28} and 5.1×10^{14} photons can produce the photo-electric effect, then the mass of a photon can be calculated to be 1.8×10^{-42} g.

Mass photon = Mass of electron / 5.1 x 10^{14} photons Mass photon = 1.8 x 10^{-42} g

What is the difference between the weight of a photon and the mass of a photon? Gravity. Thus, when an object is being measured to get the best data about it the force of gravity must be canceled in order to determine the mass. A balance works by using a fulcrum to measure mass, since the force of gravity pulls down on both sides of the balance. Both the electron and the photon move in wave form, since they are moving they have a force (force=mass x acceleration). When two objects that have the same mass and the same force strike each other what happens? Does Momentum, and its Conservation, reflect the prediction, or perhaps what you've even seen in real life? According to the conservation of momentum principle, the total amount of momentum before the photons strike the electrons is equal to the total amount afterwards—so after the energy collides they should also have a momentum of zero kg m/s. The point here is not that the photons and electrons will stop or have a momentum of zero. The objective is to get a general idea of the mass of a photon. The closer the collision is to the hypothetical momentum of zero, the closer we are to the predictable mass of a photon. Objects are going to continue to move, because zero is not equal to one. This means that a photon would have to be turned into nothing to stop it from moving. When photons collide with electrons we are not looking for zero momentum but an equal dispersion of momentum from the point of collision.

The photoelectric effect does not occur with every color of light. In an equal dispersion of momentum the particles or energy is being dispersed from a central point in all directions. This does not mean that the particles will be dispersed equally in all directions, because collisions are not always balanced. This dispersion is responsible for the photo electric effect.

The transformation between the particle (real, hard electron) and wave is really a transformation between the momentum of the electron (or another particle) and its corresponding wave. The electron must be moving to acquire momentum and a wave property. We are thus dealing with momentum—wave duality rather than particle-wave duality. When the electron is not accelerated it has no momentum and no wave properties. <http://www.hyperflight. com/primer.htm>. Since light has a mass proven by the photo-electric effect it displays a momentum-wave duality rather than a particle—wave duality.

Because the particle must be moving before its wave properties are able to manifest, a better way of seeing this mechanism is as the momentum-wave duality and not as particle-wave duality. If the electron is not accelerated, it still could be a particle but it has no wave property. So, the electron has no momentum and no wave. To make this a bit more involved—but really interesting—a moving electron may have its wave properties suppressed. (The actual electron with all of its properties is described—along with applications considerations—in the Quantum Pythagoreans book.)

So, why doesn't the electron move in set paths or straight lines? The earth orbits in a set path around the Sun. However, strong earth quakes and the China dam have shown that the earth can change its rotation slightly based on a density change. If the mass of the Earth were to change volume dramatically, then a change in the rotation of the Earth and path around the sun would change. If electrons or photons moved in set paths, would they bend easily? The bending of light makes light more difficult to break apart. Photons move in sequence one after another, changing the sequence changes the frequency. What causes the wave affect? A bowling ball will spin and produce a strike easier, if the core is not the same density throughout. (ttp://www.rotogrip. com/products/balls/ball.asp?ballid=77) A part of a custom bowling ball is made to weight more on one half to increase its curve as it moves down the lane. Photons and electrons are not equally balanced particles; a repetitive density change is occurring. How fast the repetitive change occurs depends on the frequency of photons. A higher frequency produces a shorter wavelength and a faster repetitive density change. A part of the photon must have more mass than the other part in order to produce the wave effect.

Every individual photon and every individual electron behaves the same way. Each photon (and each electron) behaves independently of all other photons (electrons). The wave representation of a moving electron or photon forms superposition (interference) pattern that is computable in accord with its own, and therefore individual, de Broglie wavelength http:// www.hyperflight.com/ primer.htm>.

What other evidence do we have that a photon has mass? Photons stay together when they are produced. A prism can be used to separate the photons. So, what keeps them so tightly joined together? Gravity is the only force we know of that is strong enough at such a small level. Gravity is the strong force that keeps the protons and neutrons together in the nucleus of an atom.

What other evidence exists that a density change in the particle produces the wave effect? The best evidence is the atom. Electrons move in orbits around the atom. They must be in control of their movement or total chaos would result. The atom is a structured system. The electron must be in control of the wave effect or energy levels would conflict. If the wave and particle were separate only one wave size would be expected. There is no other way to describe the various sizes of waves, then to conclude that the particle is altering its density to control the wavelength. Common sense would dictate that more photons would create a larger wavelength; however the opposite is what occurs. Water undergoes multiple density changes, and specific ones for changes in state; thus density changes are the mechanism the particle uses to produce the wave effect.

Why can't the mass of a photon be experimentally calculated? The best way to explain this would be to examine the difference between mass and weight. Weight is a measure of gravity on an object. The weight of an object on the moon will not be the same as the weight of the object on Earth. An astronaut weights more on earth than the moon. However, with a balance the forces of gravity are canceled, since the fulcrum is in the center of the objects being compared, like a see saw at the playground. Both objects on either side of the see saw experience the same force of gravity, so it cancels out.

We know that both the electron and the photon move in a wave form, so when they strike each other with equal mass comparisons can be made. When the same mass of water and gold are placed on opposite ends of a see saw they are in balance. If a tractor trailer smashes head on into a car, the tractor trailer will push the car violently out of the way. If a car strikes a bicyclist head on, then the bicyclist will be thrown based on the mass of the car and its acceleration. Force equals mass times acceleration, so the larger the object is the faster it is moving the greater the force. So, if two identical cars collide head on traveling with the same acceleration it is like slamming into a brick wall or coming to a complete stop. Remember the mass of the cars has not changed. Just like the mass of the electron and photon has not changed during a collision.

The stopping of an electron causes a disruption of its spin, thus producing the ejection. Why do electrons repel each other? We know that electrons move in opposite directions because they can unite like photons and increase their wavelength. This would produce an electron ejection. Thus the atom needs to prevent this from happening, so the electrons move head on in each orbital. If they strike each other, a stable product does not form just like water and oil don't mix.

So, getting a photon to rest on a balance is not going to occur. Thus, how is it certain that the mass is correct above? When trying to measure mass, the objective is to eliminate outside forces with a fulcrum. Thus get them to cancel out; since this occurs in the photo-electric effect the mass of a photon can be mathematically estimated.

Chapter 5

Human Origin Theory

Do not be afraid of those who kill the body but
cannot kill the soul. Rather, be afraid of the One
who can destroy both soul and body in hell.

Matthew 10:28

The first three chapters of the Genesis account of creation are
recorded, because the reader needs to observe that a virgin birth
or the possibility of a virgin birth in any animal is not recorded.
A theory is based on multiple problems being tested and conclusions
observed. A theory is an educated conclusion which requires belief, since
the theory could eventually change due to new observations from problems
being investigated. A theory is a belief like some believe in evolution
directly from Apes, while others believe that the law establishes origin as
the Genesis story of creation presents.

Genesis 1

[1]In the beginning God created the heaven and the earth.

[2]And the earth was without form, and void; and darkness was upon the
face of the deep. And the Spirit of God moved upon the face of the waters.

[3]And God said, Let there be light: and there was light.

⁴And God saw the light, that it was good: and God divided the light from the darkness.

⁵And God called the light Day, and the darkness he called Night. And the evening and the morning were the first day.

⁶And God said, Let there be a firmament in the midst of the waters, and let it divide the waters from the waters.

⁷And God made the firmament, and divided the waters which were under the firmament from the waters which were above the firmament: and it was so.

⁸And God called the firmament Heaven. And the evening and the morning were the second day.

⁹And God said, Let the waters under the heaven be gathered together unto one place, and let the dry land appear: and it was so.

¹⁰And God called the dry land Earth; and the gathering together of the waters called he Seas: and God saw that it was good.

¹¹And God said, Let the earth bring forth grass, the herb yielding seed, and the fruit tree yielding fruit after his kind, whose seed is in itself, upon the earth: and it was so.

¹²And the earth brought forth grass, and herb yielding seed after his kind, and the tree yielding fruit, whose seed was in itself, after his kind: and God saw that it was good.

¹³And the evening and the morning were the third day.

¹⁴And God said, Let there be lights in the firmament of the heaven to divide the day from the night; and let them be for signs, and for seasons, and for days, and years:

¹⁵And let them be for lights in the firmament of the heaven to give light upon the earth: and it was so.

¹⁶And God made two great lights; the greater light to rule the day, and the lesser light to rule the night: he made the stars also.

[17]And God set them in the firmament of the heaven to give light upon the earth,

[18]And to rule over the day and over the night, and to divide the light from the darkness: and God saw that it was good.

[19]And the evening and the morning were the fourth day.

[20]And God said, Let the waters bring forth abundantly the moving creature that hath life, and fowl that may fly above the earth in the open firmament of heaven.

[21]And God created great whales, and every living creature that moveth, which the waters brought forth abundantly, after their kind, and every winged fowl after his kind: and God saw that it was good.

[22]And God blessed them, saying, Be fruitful, and multiply, and fill the waters in the seas, and let fowl multiply in the earth.

[23]And the evening and the morning were the fifth day.

[24]And God said, Let the earth bring forth the living creature after his kind, cattle, and creeping thing, and beast of the earth after his kind: and it was so.

[25]And God made the beast of the earth after his kind, and cattle after their kind, and every thing that creepeth upon the earth after his kind: and God saw that it was good.

[26]And God said, Let us make man in our image, after our likeness: and let them have dominion over the fish of the sea, and over the fowl of the air, and over the cattle, and over all the earth, and over every creeping thing that creepeth upon the earth.

[27]So God created man in his own image, in the image of God created he him; male and female created he them.

[28]And God blessed them, and God said unto them, Be fruitful, and multiply, and replenish the earth, and subdue it: and have dominion over the fish of the sea, and over the fowl of the air, and over every living thing that moveth upon the earth.

^{29}And God said, Behold, I have given you every herb bearing seed, which is upon the face of all the earth, and every tree, in the which is the fruit of a tree yielding seed; to you it shall be for meat.

^{30}And to every beast of the earth, and to every fowl of the air, and to every thing that creepeth upon the earth, wherein there is life, I have given every green herb for meat: and it was so.

^{31}And God saw every thing that he had made, and, behold, it was very good. And the evening and the morning were the sixth day.

Genesis 2

^{1}Thus the heavens and the earth were finished, and all the host of them.

^{2}And on the seventh day God ended his work which he had made; and he rested on the seventh day from all his work which he had made.

^{3}And God blessed the seventh day, and sanctified it: because that in it he had rested from all his work which God created and made.

^{4}These are the generations of the heavens and of the earth when they were created, in the day that the LORD God made the earth and the heavens,

^{5}And every plant of the field before it was in the earth, and every herb of the field before it grew: for the LORD God had not caused it to rain upon the earth, and there was not a man to till the ground.

^{6}But there went up a mist from the earth, and watered the whole face of the ground.

^{7}And the LORD God formed man of the dust of the ground, and breathed into his nostrils the breath of life; and man became a living soul.

^{8}And the LORD God planted a garden eastward in Eden; and there he put the man whom he had formed.

^{9}And out of the ground made the LORD God to grow every tree that is pleasant to the sight, and good for food; the tree of life also in the midst of the garden, and the tree of knowledge of good and evil.

¹⁰And a river went out of Eden to water the garden; and from thence it was parted, and became into four heads.

¹¹The name of the first is Pison: that is it which compasseth the whole land of Havilah, where there is gold;

¹²And the gold of that land is good: there is bdellium and the onyx stone.

¹³And the name of the second river is Gihon: the same is it that compasseth the whole land of Ethiopia.

¹⁴And the name of the third river is Hiddekel: that is it which goeth toward the east of Assyria. And the fourth river is Euphrates.

¹⁵And the LORD God took the man, and put him into the garden of Eden to dress it and to keep it.

¹⁶And the LORD God commanded the man, saying, Of every tree of the garden thou mayest freely eat:

¹⁷But of the tree of the knowledge of good and evil, thou shalt not eat of it: for in the day that thou eatest thereof thou shalt surely die.

¹⁸And the LORD God said, It is not good that the man should be alone; I will make him an help meet for him.

¹⁹And out of the ground the LORD God formed every beast of the field, and every fowl of the air; and brought them unto Adam to see what he would call them: and whatsoever Adam called every living creature, that was the name thereof.

²⁰And Adam gave names to all cattle, and to the fowl of the air, and to every beast of the field; but for Adam there was not found an help meet for him.

²¹And the LORD God caused a deep sleep to fall upon Adam, and he slept: and he took one of his ribs, and closed up the flesh instead thereof;

²²And the rib, which the LORD God had taken from man, made he a woman, and brought her unto the man.

²³And Adam said, This is now bone of my bones, and flesh of my flesh: she shall be called Woman, because she was taken out of Man.

²⁴Therefore shall a man leave his father and his mother, and shall cleave unto his wife: and they shall be one flesh.

²⁵And they were both naked, the man and his wife, and were not ashamed.

Genesis 3

¹Now the serpent was more subtil than any beast of the field which the LORD God had made. And he said unto the woman, Yea, hath God said, Ye shall not eat of every tree of the garden?

²And the woman said unto the serpent, We may eat of the fruit of the trees of the garden:

³But of the fruit of the tree which is in the midst of the garden, God hath said, Ye shall not eat of it, neither shall ye touch it, lest ye die.

⁴And the serpent said unto the woman, Ye shall not surely die:

⁵For God doth know that in the day ye eat thereof, then your eyes shall be opened, and ye shall be as gods, knowing good and evil.

⁶And when the woman saw that the tree was good for food, and that it was pleasant to the eyes, and a tree to be desired to make one wise, she took of the fruit thereof, and did eat, and gave also unto her husband with her; and he did eat.

⁷And the eyes of them both were opened, and they knew that they were naked; and they sewed fig leaves together, and made themselves aprons.

⁸And they heard the voice of the LORD God walking in the garden in the cool of the day: and Adam and his wife hid themselves from the presence of the LORD God amongst the trees of the garden.

⁹And the LORD God called unto Adam, and said unto him, Where art thou?

¹⁰And he said, I heard thy voice in the garden, and I was afraid, because I was naked; and I hid myself.

[11]And he said, Who told thee that thou wast naked? Hast thou eaten of the tree, whereof I commanded thee that thou shouldest not eat?

[12]And the man said, The woman whom thou gavest to be with me, she gave me of the tree, and I did eat.

[13]And the LORD God said unto the woman, What is this that thou hast done? And the woman said, The serpent beguiled me, and I did eat.

[14]And the LORD God said unto the serpent, Because thou hast done this, thou art cursed above all cattle, and above every beast of the field; upon thy belly shalt thou go, and dust shalt thou eat all the days of thy life:

[15]And I will put enmity between thee and the woman, and between thy seed and her seed; it shall bruise thy head, and thou shalt bruise his heel.

[16]Unto the woman he said, I will greatly multiply thy sorrow and thy conception; in sorrow thou shalt bring forth children; and thy desire shall be to thy husband, and he shall rule over thee.

[17]And unto Adam he said, Because thou hast hearkened unto the voice of thy wife, and hast eaten of the tree, of which I commanded thee, saying, Thou shalt not eat of it: cursed is the ground for thy sake; in sorrow shalt thou eat of it all the days of thy life;

When did Evolution begin?

- Jewish, Muslim, Christians—after the fall of Adam and Eve (Genesis 3:1-17)

- Theists, Buddhists—We believe that God could have known every event of the future had God decided to create a fully determined universe. Animals can reincarnate from one animal to another based on rewards. Since the universe is not determined, then evolution has occurred randomly since its beginning.

- Atheists—Science has not proven something to be perfect, thus evolution occurs randomly and began on the Earth or came from outer space more than a billion years ago.

After the fall of Adam and Eve the majority of religious scholars believe micro-evolution began. Micro-evolution concerns gene changes in an organism, and an example would be breading wheat to produce a larger seed. Macro-evolution concerns chromosome changes and concerns a change in species, since a species must have the same chromosome number in order to produce an offspring that can reproduce.

A virgin birth occurs by increasing the chromosomal number, thus it is a macro-evolution change. Any change in the chromosome is associated with macro-evolution. Meiosis is the process where the chromosome number will increase and then divide into haploid chromosomes. A haploid is a single chromosome which during sexual reproduction one will travel in the sperm to meet up with one in the egg. In a virgin birth the haploid chromosome number doubles or becomes a diploid in a genetic controlled process. The specific gene sequence responsible for the virgin birth process has not yet been recorded, however it does exist because the virgin birth has been documented in both the Komodo dragon and Zebra shark.

Since a virgin birth is not mentioned in the genesis story of creation and it has been documented as occurring in a zebra shark and komodo dragons, then a virgin birth represents an evolutionary birth. Creation represents an automatic birth or a birth that occurred quickly out of dust. An evolutionary birth is one that occurs over a longer period of time, such as Mary the mother of Jesus where her baby took multiple months to fully develop before live birth. It is documented that Mary moved around while pregnant and Joseph did not leave her because he was told of her virgin birth in a dream. (Matthew 1:19-20)

This leads to the following question: Can sin produce a child pure at birth? The Pharisee and Sadducees struggled with Jesus Christ's birth because of the premise that the fall of Adam and Eve produced death and changes in DNA. Even the Catholic Church struggles with this issue, since they view Mary as being sinless described by the term immaculate conception. This is significant based on what Jesus told Peter about the foundation of the Church being built upon the rock.

If Adam and Eve were conceived by a virgin birth from lower animals that evolved over many years, how would the creation story fit into this scenario?

What is the creation story all about? What is the purpose of the creation story? Why are we here on the planet?

The primary purpose of the creation story is to begin the process to define the meaning of life. Why does life exist? What is our purpose for this life? Why are we here? Does life have meaning?

The primary goal of the Genesis account of creation is to define God's creative ability, identify the fallen arch angel Genesis 37:34-35, Matthew 10:28, and to state God's plan for our existence.

If you are upset with the whole idea of evolution and virgin births, then I can't wait till you meet Jesus Christ. God can and does define the meaning of life by virgin birth! Jesus Christ provides us with the opportunity to become a child of God. This is the meaning of life.

Evolution is defined as change over time; and occurs based on the following: Mutation of DNA, Adaptation of the genetic change, and Natural Selection or fighting for a place to live. Micro-Evolution concerns gene changes and there are countless experiments that prove this occurs in living cells. Macro-Evolution concerns chromosomal changes; chromosomal nondisjunctions provide evidence that chromosomes do change in number.

Charles Darwin published a book called The Origin of Species. The primary point of the book is that Humans evolved directly from lower animals. According to the Torah, this is heresy. (Deut. 13:1-4) All those who teach this view to others are heretics. Humans are distinctly different compared to other animals; the best evidence for the Creation story is found in Law and Government. We are the most advanced animal on the planet; no animal is mocking our behavior to establish a moral and just government. Our justice system blatantly affirms the stance that we did not evolve from an insane animal. If we continue to educate our children to think that we came from an insane animal; then subconsciously why would they desire to learn to obey laws that have no merit based on the Torah?

There are some problems with this view of our origin as stated in Charles Darwin's book. The following is a list of the problems:

1. If the organism is sexual, then it would have to produce both a male and female with the same chromosomal change in order to produce an off spring as a new species. How would a species know to do that? This definitely would not be a random event, since very few animals are hermaphrodites so the process would need to be timed exactly.

2. A government can't be founded on evolution. Evolution is founded on the following three principles: Mutation, Adaptation, and Natural Selection. Natural Selection concerns the survival of the strongest with no restrictions to prevent lying, murder, stealing, or rape. Survival of the fittest makes life in the jungle wild. In the jungle, is it easy for younger animals to steal food or territory from older animals? Should it be legal for young adults to steal from older adults? Our government prevents natural selection by taxing the rich or strong and giving to the poor or weak. How? Taking from the rich and giving to the poor thwarts Natural Selection. Also, murder and stealing are prevented by the government which is in contradiction with the principles of evolution. Evidence, Hitler tried to establish the perfect human race under the principles of natural selection. He lied to the Jews by telling them they were going to take a shower. He took the innocent life or murdered many Jewish people in gas chambers that looked like showers; he stole their territory and valuables. According to evolution the poor weak humans should not be helped, since the weak do not play a role in the survival of the species.

3. Hitler tried to establish a government on evolution and was proven to be a failure and defeated even though he tried to keep his plans for the perfect race secret. Scientists think in terms of origin and elected leaders think in terms of Law. Lastly, the very foundation of our legal system would fall apart based on evolution. Why? Evolution from insane animals prevents a legal system from establishing justice. It's all about accountability. The Genesis account of Creation is founded on this principle. Adam and Eve in this account are created sinless, which means that they understood the difference between what is good and what is bad. An insane animal does not know the difference. Adult Homo sapiens can't blame apes that are insane as the reason they committed a crime in court, because they would be implying equality; since science has proven that some behaviors are learned and some are inherited. If humans randomly evolved from apes, then the majority would still have the inherited insanity behavior and establishing a justice system would be dubious. An adult could

easily argue that Homo sapiens have not existed on Earth long enough for these genes to have all become recessive. Our justice system blatantly affirms the stance that humans did not come from an insane animal.

4. Random evolution from dust to ape, then a human is the basis for the establishment of a religion. How? Random evolution sets up a system of beliefs that this is what happened, even though no one was there to witness the event and the human should be worshiped or rewarded with any pleasure that is fulfilling. King and Queen of the jungle describes the religion that justifies the behavior of those who believe in random evolution from dust to ape. For example, Atheism is a religion in which people choose to believe there is no God in charge. If nothing has power over God, then randomness is infinite and perfection is impossible. The goal of Atheism is to convince people that "Nothing" has power over "Something", because "Nothing" is God. "Nothing" is perfect, since it is dependent on "Something".

The question is which God do you choose to serve? This is the reason our God is a jealous God. Serving "Nothing" is the opposite of believing in God found in the Creation account. Why should I put up with Atheism being forced upon me? Their idea is to promote randomness as the power associated with Creation, since "Nothing" is not capable of having a plan. Atheists love evolution as it is taught because it has errors associated with it. The corner stone of our government is not evolution. Thus that is at least one error associated with evolution. Randomness always has an error associated with a problem. However, Atheists only see "Nothing" as perfection; that is why they believe in "Nothing" and not "Something". Something to an Atheist has errors associated with it, since they don't believe in the Creation Story! Therefore, the doctrine of Atheism indicates that problems always have an error associated with an outcome, since perfection is impossible.

What about the fossil evidence that supports Human evolution? Principles of human evolution from an insane species require a virgin birth of Adam and Eve for the establishment of a moral and just human government (Isaiah 9:6). According to the Torah this would be classified as Heresy. (Deut. 13:1-4) A virgin birth is not an out of the box event. A Komodo dragon can produce a virgin birth, if kept in captivity. (http:// news. nationalgeographic.com/news/2006/12/061220-virgin-dragons. html) There are other documented cases; however none of a mammal other than that of Jesus Christ. Whichever conclusion the reader makes, our origin was a unique event because other animals don't understand the difference between what is right and wrong. Moreover any conclusion that is reached concerning our origin will establish a religion.

Both modern man and Neanderthal man shared the same mother, since they were capable of mating and produced offspring. It was once thought that Modern Man (Homo sapiens sapiens) began with the arrival of Cro-Magnon man in Europe about 40,000 years ago. However, current thinking, based on archaeological finds and genetic studies of mutations of mitochondrial DNA in populations of different people of the world, is that Modern Man evolved in Africa about 190,000 years ago, moved into the Middle East by 120,000 years ago, then into Asia, and on to Australia at least 60,000 years ago. This was at a time when Neanderthal man was the dominant hominid in parts of Europe. Modern Man later moved into Europe about 40,000 years ago and into the American continent about 14,000 years ago. While other world cultures developed and changed, the Australians remained relatively isolated on their island continent. The longest continuing religion in the world belongs to Australia's Aborigines, with the Rainbow Serpent mythology recorded in rock shelter paintings believed to be 7,000 years old in the Kakadu National Park region, where this Ancestral Being is still important to local people.

The Ngaanyatjarra language group is located in the Western Desert region of Western Australia. The overview is derived from Into another World: A Glimpse of the Culture of the Ngaanyatjarra People. Traditionally, Ngaanyatjarra people do not celebrate birthdays or count years for the purpose of calculating age. Ngaanyatjarra, like many traditional Aboriginal languages, has no formal system of quantification (numbers, time, distance, quantity etc). The main point here is that Biology, the science that is the study of life has chosen to ignore this evidence in support of an infinite universe.

The archaeological evidence revealed that the earliest Neanderthals had lived in Europe about 200,000 years ago. But then, about 30,000 years ago, they disappeared. About 45,000 years ago, the climate of Europe went through a burst of very sudden switches between warm and cold conditions that would have transformed the Neanderthals' environment. Anthropology professor Leslie Aiello from UCL, teamed up with Dr George Havenith, who runs a laboratory studying the way modern humans retain heat at Loughborough University. They subjected two modern humans with very different body shapes to cooling in an ice bath. One had the long limbed, athletic shape of a runner, the other had a stockier, heavily-muscled body plan closer to that of a Neanderthal. The heavily muscled person lasted longer in the ice bath, so it seems that Neanderthal would have had an advantage. His muscle would have acted as an insulator, and his deep chest did help to keep organs warm.

The forests on which they depended began to recede, giving way to open plains. On these plains, Professor Shea believes, the Neanderthal thrusting spear and ambush strategy wouldn't have worked. So Neanderthals retreated with the forests, their population falling as their hunting grounds shrank. By comparison, modern humans made lighter stone points that could be fitted on to lighter spear shafts. These could be thrown, enabling our ancestors to hunt more effectively in an open landscape. Hunting in an open landscape also required high levels of mobility to follow migrating herds, and the agility to throw the spears themselves. For Neanderthal, it was an ironic end. The very body plan that had made Neanderthal so well adapted to the Ice Age, had locked him into an evolutionary cul-de-sac. He might have been better adapted to the cold than the first modern humans, but as the landscape changed, it was our ancestors, who could take better advantage of the more open environment, who survived.

Neanderthals most likely came from Africa, as many skeletons have been found in the Levant. Modern humans (Homo sapiens) seem to also have all come from Africa. Most scholars believe Ethiopia is the cradle of life. In 2010, scientists completed the first sequence of the Neanderthal genome using DNA extracted from fossils, and an examination of the genetic material suggested that modern humans' ancestors occasionally successfully interbred with Neanderthals. Recent estimates reveal that Neanderthal DNA makes up 1 percent to 4 percent of modern Eurasian genomes, perhaps endowing some people with the robust immune systems they enjoy today.

The Neanderthal genome revealed that people outside Africa share more genetic variants with Neanderthals than Africans do. One possible explanation is that modern humans mixed with Neanderthals after the modern lineage began appearing outside Africa at least 100,000 years ago.

Another, more complex scenario is that an African group ancestral to both Neanderthals and certain modern human populations genetically diverged from other Africans beginning about 230,000 years ago. This group then stayed genetically distinct until it eventually left Africa.

To shed light on why Neanderthals appear most closely related to people outside Africa, researchers looked at similar DNA chunks in European and Neanderthal genomes. When sperm and egg cells are created, the strands of DNA within them break and rejoin to form new combinations of genetic material. This "recombination" decreases the length of the chunks in each generation. By comparing lengths, "we can estimate when the two populations last shared genes," explained researcher Sriram Sankararaman, a statistical geneticist at Harvard Medical School.

The research team estimates modern humans and Neanderthals last exchanged genes between 37,000 and 86,000 years ago, and most likely 47,000 to 65,000 years ago. This is well after modern humans began expanding outside Africa, but potentially before they started spreading across Eurasia.

These findings suggest modern humans last shared ancestors with Neanderthals during the period known as the Upper Paleolithic. http://www.livescience.com/23730-neanderthals-modern-humans-interbreeding.html

Modern Humans and Neanderthals could mate, which means that they came from the same mother. In order for an offspring to be viable, which means for it to be capable of reproduction the original parents had to have the same number of chromosomes. A male with 46 chromosomes can mate with a female with 46 chromosomes and produce offspring. A male with 46 chromosomes can't mate and produce offspring with another animal with a different number. This behavior is known as beasitality as Leviticus 20:15 states it has occurred more than once, and it still occurs today documented in the porn industry.

Bacteria do not have chromosomes, thus the transition from circular DNA to chromosomal has not been determined. Why is the virgin birth gene important? Bacteria have circular DNA and only single copies of their DNA in each cell.

The transition from bacteria with one copy of genetic info into sexual reproduction with two copies resulted from the virgin birth gene. It is the only way for this process to increase the number of chromosomes in a cell without originally starting with two copies of genetic information. What does this mean? The step from asexual reproduction to sexual reproduction requires an increase in the chromosomal number from one copy to two copies. Thus the virgin birth gene is responsible for every organism that reproduces by sexual reproduction, since it started the process.

The virgin birth gene is responsible for making Meiosis possible. In many organisms, including all animals and land plants (but not some other groups such as fungi), gametes are called sperm and egg cells. Meiosis begins with one diploid cell containing two copies of each chromosome— one from the organism's mother and one from its father. The cell divides twice, potentially producing up to four haploid cells containing one copy of each chromosome. ("Potentially" because in some cases, such as the formation of oocytes in mammals, only one of the possible four haploid cells survives.) In animals the haploid cell resulting from meiosis is a male or female gamete. Each of the resulting chromosomes in the gamete cells is a unique mixture of maternal and paternal DNA, resulting in offspring that are genetically distinct from either parent. This gives rise to genetic diversity in sexually reproducing populations. This genetic diversity can provide the variation of physical and behavioral attributes (phenotypes) upon which natural selection can act.

The virgin birth gene is the "father" of both Mitosis and Meiosis, because neither would exist without this gene. During Interphase the synthesis of DNA occurs and once complete the process of mitosis occurs leading to cytokinesis or cell division. Also, DNA synthesis occurs in circular DNA before prokaryotes like bacteria undergo cell division. The significance of the virgin birth gene concerns its ability to stop the process of cell division after DNA synthesis occurs. **This is the first step towards the production of chromosomes, because they occur in pairs.** The virgin birth gene has the ability to stop cell division which would prevent the formation of two haploid cells. The ability of the gene to stop cell division allows the virgin birth to occur. Thus the virgin birth gene in circular bacterial DNA would promote replication without cell division creating the diploid cell. Once the diploid cell is produced, then interphase can start and Mitosis can occur. Interphase increases the pair of chromosomes to four copies and then Mitosis occurs.

The organism with the least number of chromosomes is the male Australian ant, Myrmecia pilosula, with one chromosome per cell. Male ants are generally haploid-that is, they have half the number of normal chromosomes-while the female ant has two chromosomes per cell. Bacteria have one circular chromosome consisting of DNA and associated proteins. The virgin birth gene is responsible for separating the Australian ant from the Nostoc Punctiforme bacteria.

The virgin birth gene is so significant, since it is also responsible for the creation of the chromosome. If it can read it, then it can create it since it knows where to start and stop the process. It can produce a chromosome from another, so it has the steps necessary in the gene to build a chromosome from a circular DNA strand once the strand has been duplicated and two copies are not present. Moreover, the most important part concerns the division that does not occur after the replication or second copy is produced in the prokaryote according to evolution from single cells.

Jesus did not come to pressure people into a religion. The purpose of the author is not to create a wave, but to prepare the way. Creating a wave would be to say that the Bible should be changed, that the Genesis story should include an evolution of life from bacteria to ape, then the virgin birth of Adam and Eve. This is not the objective of the author, nor would the author support any change to the Genesis story. To change the Genesis story would eventually produce a society that would question whether Jesus was really crucified by the Jews and the Roman government. No different than the Jews questioning whether Jesus rose from the grave and creating lies to cover up the truth. The Genesis story is about trusting in God, and those hear the truth and support it are the children of God. Moreover, Jesus did not come to pressure people into a religion, he came to reconcile with us over the punishment of death. This is the reason Human Evolution should not be taught in the public education system, since it will set up a religion that humans will use for the purpose of profit. It is a choice to accept Jesus as your lord and savior. Why is this important? Jesus spoke about it in a parable of the talents. It is a choice to use the talents you have been given, and I have no desire to suppress choice because of the creativity and diversity that it produces. Choice clearly allows the enemy to be defined. (Matthew 5:44)

A Jewish Priest was the smartest person in the tribe and studied to promote the truth. Problems were studied by the Priests and decisions made and proven in battle with victory. Human evolution was battle tested in World War II as Hitler tried to establish the perfect human race. World War

II would be documented evidence for the Jewish race to never embrace human evolution by changing the Torah to account for our origin on this planet. A virgin birth is an evolutionary birth, since it occurs in several different species and results in a change in chromosomal number. The Komodo dragon is an example of where it occurs. According to evolution, many different species use the same gene. Thus genes can be carried between species and function properly. A virgin birth is a detailed sequence of replication and organization, thus a virgin birth would require a virgin birth gene Therefore the principles of human evolution from an insane species require a virgin birth of Adam and Eve for the establishment of a moral and just human government (Isaiah 9:6).

Humans are more complex than other animals. Thus apes would not develop computers over an unlimited period of time, since their brain is limited in size due to the muscle strength associated with eating.

Abiogenesis or biopoiesis is a natural process from which life arises from simple organic compounds. In a recent Nova Science Now episode Neil Degrasse Tyson explains how a chemist has designed a natural process to assemble and create the building blocks of life. http://www.pbs.org/wgbh/nova/evolution/where-did-we-come-from.html This is significant, because it shows that nonliving elements are capable of producing an organized structure that is capable of reproduction. The point here is that something must be organized at its core in order to be capable of the production of something else that is complex. If something and nothing are opposites, then complex protein structures would not exist.

Science currently promotes matter and energy evolving from nothing randomly. Unfortunately this would never occur, since nothing lacks the basic structure (nothing means void of anything) to build upon. For nothing to create something out of emptiness would produce a system that would allow Adenine to bond with Guanine, since opposites would not exist. Life would never evolve under these circumstances, because complex structures would be impossible to assemble. Currently, science promotes evolution as a random occurrence because it does not view something as organized and eternal. The PBS documentary showing a natural process to assemble and create the building blocks of life provides evidence that something is organized and did not randomly put elements together to create the building blocks of life. To assemble a puzzle the pieces must fit together in the design that they were cut, thus DNA follows this same pattern with Adenine and Tyrosine, Guanine and Cytosine, and Adenine and Uracil specifically bonding together. Adenine and Guanine will not fit together to create a building block of life. Order and structure are associated with something, since it has mass and the ability to maintain order.

The miracles Jesus performed add credibility to those who followed him. Jesus was a Jew and as a Jew he was held accountable to the Torah. Using the Torah, Priests accused Jesus of being a Blasphemer and a Heretic. The Torah states that all mitzvot remain binding forever, and anyone coming to change the Torah is immediately identified as a false prophet. (Deut. 13:1-4) Throughout the New Testament, Jesus contradicts the Torah and states that its commandments are no longer applicable. (Rabbi Shraga Simmons) For Heresy, John 9:14 records that Jesus made a paste in violation of Shabbat, which caused the Pharisees to say (verse 16); "He does not observe Shabbat!" If you contradict the Torah, then that is Heresy. Jesus claim to be the Messiah and, in fact, to have majesty and authority belonging only to God was therefore regarded by Caiaphas as blasphemy which the Mosaic Law prescribed death by stoning (Lev24:16). (Mark 14:64)

One of the most common questions received at Aish.com is: "Why don't Jews believe in Jesus?" Let's understand why—not in order to to disparage other religions, but rather to clarify the Jewish position.

Jews do not accept Jesus as the messiah because:

Jesus did not fulfill the messianic prophecies. Jesus did not embody the personal qualifications of the Messiah. Biblical verses "referring" to Jesus are mistranslations. Jewish belief is based on national revelation. But first, some background: What exactly is the Messiah?

The word "Messiah" is an English rendering of the Hebrew word *"Mashiach"*, which means "Anointed." It usually refers to a person initiated into God's service by being anointed with oil. (Exodus 29:7, I Kings 1:39, II Kings 9:3)

Since every King and High Priest was anointed with oil, each may be referred to as "an anointed one" (a *Mashiach* or a Messiah). For example: "God forbid that I [David] should stretch out my hand against the Lord's Messiah [Saul] . . ." (I Samuel 26:11. Cf. II Samuel 23:1, Isaiah 45:1, Psalms 20:6)

Where does the Jewish concept of Messiah come from? One of the central themes of Biblical prophecy is the promise of a future age of perfection characterized by universal peace and recognition of God. (Isaiah 2:1-4; Zephaniah 3:9; Hosea 2:20-22; Amos 9:13-15; Isaiah 32:15-18, 60:15-18; Micah 4:1-4; Zechariah 8:23, 14:9; Jeremiah 31:33-34)

Many of these prophetic passages speak of a descendant of King David who will rule Israel during the age of perfection. (Isaiah 11:1-9; Jeremiah 23:5-6, 30:7-10, 33:14-16; Ezekiel 34:11-31, 37:21-28; Hosea 3:4-5)

Since every King is a Messiah, by convention, we refer to this future anointed king as *The* Messiah. The above is the only description in the Bible of a Davidic descendant who is to come in the future. We will recognize the Messiah by seeing who the King of Israel is at the time of complete universal perfection.

Jesus Did Not Fulfill the Messianic Prophecies

What is the Messiah supposed to accomplish? The Bible says that he will:

- Build the Third Temple (Ezekiel 37:26-28).

- Gather all Jews back to the Land of Israel (Isaiah 43:5-6).

- Usher in an era of world peace, and end all hatred, oppression, suffering and disease. As it says: "Nation shall not lift up sword against nation, neither shall man learn war anymore." (Isaiah 2:4)

- Spread universal knowledge of the God of Israel, which will unite humanity as one. As it says: "God will be King over all the world—on that day, God will be One and His Name will be One" (Zechariah 14:9).

If an individual fails to fulfill even one of these conditions, then he cannot be "The Messiah."

Because no one has ever fulfilled the Bible's description of this future King, Jews still await the coming of the Messiah. All past Messianic claimants, including Jesus of Nazareth, Bar Cochba and Shabbtai Tzvi have been rejected.

Christians counter that Jesus will fulfill these in the Second Coming, but Jewish sources show that the Messiah will fulfill the prophecies outright; in the Bible no concept of a second coming exists.

Jesus Did Not Embody the Personal Qualifications of Messiah

Messiah as Prophet

The Messiah will become the greatest prophet in history, second only to Moses. (Targum—Isaiah 11:2; Maimonides—Yad Teshuva 9:2)

Prophecy can only exist in Israel when the land is inhabited by a majority of world Jewry, a situation which has not existed since 300 BCE. During the time of Ezra, when the majority of Jews refused to move from Babylon to Israel, prophecy ended upon the death of the last prophets—Haggai, Zechariah and Malachi.

Jesus was not a prophet; he appeared on the scene approximately 350 years after prophecy had ended.

Descendent of David

According to Jewish sources, the Messiah will be born of human parents and possess normal physical attributes like other people. He will not be a demi-god, (1) nor will he possess supernatural qualities.

The Messiah must be descended on his father's side from King David (see Genesis 49:10, Isaiah 11:1, Jeremiah 23:5, 33:17; Ezekiel 34:23-24). According to the Christian claim that Jesus was the product of a virgin birth, he had no father—and thus could not have possibly fulfilled the messianic requirement of being descended on his father's side from King David. (2)

Torah Observance

The Messiah will lead the Jewish people to full Torah observance. The Torah states that all mitzvot remain binding forever, and anyone coming to change the Torah is immediately identified as a false prophet. (Deut. 13:1-4)

Throughout the New Testament, Jesus contradicts the Torah and states that its commandments are no longer applicable. For example, John 9:14 records that Jesus made a paste in violation of Shabbat, which caused the Pharisees to say (verse 16), "He does not observe Shabbat!"

Mistranslated Verses "Referring" to Jesus

Biblical verses can only be understood by studying the original Hebrew text—which reveals many discrepancies in the Christian translation.

Virgin Birth

The Christian idea of a virgin birth is derived from the verse in Isaiah 7:14 describing an *"alma"* as giving birth. The word *"alma"* has always meant a young woman, but Christian theologians came centuries later and translated it as "virgin." This accords Jesus' birth with the first century pagan idea of mortals being impregnated by gods.

Suffering Servant

Christianity claims that Isaiah chapter 53 refers to Jesus, as the "suffering servant."

In actuality, Isaiah 53 directly follows the theme of chapter 52, describing the exile and redemption of the Jewish people. The prophecies are written in the singular form because the Jews ("Israel") are regarded as one unit. Throughout Jewish scripture, Israel is repeatedly called, in the singular, the "Servant of God" (see Isaiah 43:8). In fact, Isaiah states no less than 11 times in the chapters prior to 53 that the Servant of God is Israel. When read correctly, Isaiah 53 clearly [and ironically] refers to the Jewish people being "bruised, crushed and as sheep brought to slaughter" at the hands of the nations of the world. These descriptions are used throughout Jewish scripture to graphically describe the suffering of the Jewish people (see Psalm 44). Isaiah 53 concludes that when the Jewish people are redeemed, the nations will recognize and accept responsibility for the inordinate suffering and death of the Jews.

Jewish Belief is Based Solely on National Revelation

Throughout history, thousands of religions have been started by individuals, attempting to convince people that he or she is God's true prophet. But personal revelation is an extremely weak basis for a religion because one can never know if it is indeed true. Since others did not hear God speak to this person, they have to take his word for it. Even if the individual claiming personal revelation performs miracles, there is still no verification that he is a genuine prophet. Miracles do not prove anything. All they show—assuming they are genuine—is that he has certain powers. It has nothing to do with his claim of prophecy.

Judaism, unique among all of the world's major religions, does not rely on "claims of miracles" as the basis for its religion. In fact, the Bible says that God sometimes grants the power of "miracles" to charlatans, in order to test Jewish loyalty to the Torah (Deut. 13:4).

Of the thousands of religions in human history, only Judaism bases its belief on national revelation—i.e. God speaking to the entire nation. If God is going to start a religion, it makes sense He'll tell everyone, not just one person.

Maimonides states (Foundations of Torah, ch. 8):

> *The Jews did not believe in Moses, our teacher, because of the miracles he performed. Whenever anyone's belief is based on seeing miracles, he has lingering doubts, because it is possible the miracles were performed through magic or sorcery. All of the miracles performed by Moses in the desert were because they were necessary, and not as proof of his prophecy.*

> *What then was the basis of [Jewish] belief? The Revelation at Mount Sinai, which we saw with our own eyes and heard with our own ears, not dependent on the testimony of others . . . as it says, "Face to face, God spoke with you . . ." The Torah also states: "God did not make this covenant with our fathers, but with us—who are all here alive today." (Deut. 5:3)*

Judaism is not miracles. It is the personal eyewitness experience of every man, woman and child, standing at Mount Sinai 3,300 years ago.

For further reading: "Did God Speak at Mount Sinai?"

Waiting for the Messiah

The world is in desperate need of Messianic redemption. And to the extent we are aware of the problems of society, is the extent we will yearn for redemption. As the Talmud says, one of the first questions asked of a Jew on Judgment Day is: "Did you yearn for the arrival of the Messiah?"

How can we hasten the coming of the Messiah? The best way is to love all humanity generously, to keep the mitzvot of the Torah (as best we can), and to encourage others to do so as well.

Despite the gloom, the world does seem headed toward redemption. One apparent sign is that the Jewish people have returned to the Land of Israel and made it bloom again. Additionally, a major movement is afoot of young Jews returning to Torah tradition.

The Messiah can come any day, and it all depends on our actions. God is ready when we are. For as King David says: "Redemption will come today—if you hearken to His voice."

For further study:

Jews for Judaism

- "The Real Messiah," by Rabbi Aryeh Kaplan

- "Let's Get Biblical! Why Doesn't Judaism Accept the Christian Messiah?," by Rabbi Tovia Singer

- "The Path of the Righteous Gentile," by Chaim Clorfene and Yakov Rogalsky

FOOTNOTES

Maimonides devotes much of the "Guide for the Perplexed" to the fundamental idea that God is incorporeal, meaning that He assumes no physical form. God is Eternal, above time. He is Infinite, beyond space. He cannot be born, and cannot die. Saying that God assumes human form makes God small, diminishing both His unity and His divinity. As the Torah says: "God is not a mortal" (Numbers 23:19).

In response, it is claimed that Joseph adopted Jesus, and passed on his genealogy via adoption. There are two problems with this claim:

There is no Biblical basis for the idea of a father passing on his tribal line by adoption. A priest who adopts a son from another tribe cannot make him a priest by adoption;

Joseph could never pass on by adoption that which he doesn't have. Because Joseph descended from Jeconiah (Matthew 1:11) he fell under the curse of that king that none of his descendants could ever sit as king upon the throne of David. (Jeremiah 22:30; 36:30)

To answer this difficult problem, apologists claim that Jesus traces himself back to King David through his mother Mary, who allegedly descends from David, as shown in the third chapter of Luke. There are four basic problems with this claim:

There is no evidence that Mary descends from David. The third chapter of Luke traces Joseph's genealogy, not Mary's. Even if Mary can trace herself back to David, that doesn't help Jesus, since tribal affiliation goes only through the father, not mother. Cf. Numbers 1:18; Ezra 2:59.

Even if family line could go through the mother, Mary was not from a legitimate Messianic family. According to the Bible, the Messiah must be a descendent of David through his son Solomon (II Samuel 7:14; I Chronicles 17:11-14, 22:9-10, 28:4-6). The third chapter of Luke is irrelevant to this discussion because it describes lineage of David's son Nathan, not Solomon. (Luke 3:31)

Luke 3:27 lists Shealtiel and Zerubbabel in his genealogy. These two also appear in Matthew 1:12 as descendants of the cursed Jeconiah. If Mary descends from them, it would also disqualify her from being a Messianic progenitor. (http://www.aish.com)

When Charles Darwin published his book The Origin of Species, he was instantly labeled as promoting Heresy based on the fact that the book does not support the teachings of the Torah. Any person that teaches what Charles Darwin believes is a Heretic for promoting Heresy. If an individual picks any part of the Torah and says it is not true, then he or she affirms the whole Torah is not true. A follower of the Torah must support all of it to not be labeled as a Heretic.

If the author had published this book during the time of Jesus, he would have been charged with Heresy and put to death for supporting the teachings of Jesus Christ. Even though I personally have done nothing physically (I was not born by virgin birth) that would support a documented change in the Torah, however I am still labeled as a Heretic because I am teaching others about Jesus Christ.

THE TWELVE APOSTLES:

- Andrew—crucified

- Bartholomew—beaten then crucified

- James, son of Alphaeus—stoned to death

- James, son of Zebedee—beheaded

- John—exiled for his faith; died of old age

- Judas (not Iscariot)—stoned to death

- Matthew—speared to death

- Peter—crucified upside down

- Philip—crucified

- Simon—crucified

- Thomas—speared to death

  atthias—stoned to death (http://www.reclaimingthemind. org/blog/2007/09/what-happened-to-the-twelve-apostles/)

Kentucky has the only Creation museum in the world; however the creator of the museum is a Heretic. He is a Heretic, because he is a believer in Jesus and supports his teachings. Just supporting 99percent of the Torah is not enough to not be labeled by it as a Heretic. Peter was crucified upside down as a reminder to us that hind sight is 20/20. It is not easy to take risks when the odds seem so great against the plan succeeding. David took a risk and killed Goliath and the Philistines from that day forward wanted David dead. David fought with the sword and in sleeping with Bathsheba concluded that he had no peace. Forgiveness produces peace and without forgiveness only more war is expected, because Jesus stated those who live by the sword die by the sword just before he was crucified. To be crucified naked upside down would be a horrible way to die and any sane person would fight to the death to prevent being tortured publicly in front of others who lived a more visible life of sin.

The torah has laws associated with performing a sacrifice. Those laws were not followed in the sacrifice of Jesus Christ. Jesus was brutally beaten and nailed to a cross. Should the Torah be changes, since Jesus said its laws are no longer applicable? The Torah should not be changed, since changing it would make it difficult to understand the brutality associated with the sacrifice of Jesus Christ. If the Torah is absolutely perfect, then it becomes a god worthy of being worshiped, just like an asherah pole or golden calf. The author has no intention of making the Bible perfect, because in a matter of time people would choose to worship a book and kill those who try to burn it instead of loving them as Jesus commands in the second greatest commandment.

Man does not tell God what is good or what to do. The Torah is worthy of praise; Jesus stated this when he made scripture references to it. He showed us what our Father had placed in the Torah on Mt. Sinai. Jesus explained the summary this way: Jesus taught, Mt 22:37 "You shall love the Lord your God with all your heart, and with all your soul, and with all your mind. This is the great and first commandment. And a second is like it, you shall love your neighbor as yourself. On these two commandments all the law and the prophets are founded." However, he was labeled as a Heretic. The Torah states that all mitzvot remain binding forever, and anyone coming to change the Torah is immediately identified as a false prophet. (Deut. 13:1-4)

Let us look at the Scripture. Deut 13:1-4 "If a prophet arises among you, or a dreamer of dreams, and gives you a sign or a wonder, and the sign or wonder which he tells you comes to pass, and if he says, 'Let us go after other gods,' which you have not known, 'and let us serve them,' you shall not listen to the words of that prophet or to that dreamer of dreams; for the Lord your God is testing you, to know whether you love the Lord your God with all your heart and with all your soul. You shall walk after the Lord your God and fear him, and keep his commandments and obey his voice, and you shall serve him and cleave to him."

If the Pharisees had been *tzaddikim*, holy sages, we might have to take their analysis seriously. However, Jesus pointed out that they had become corrupt. Mt 15:1 "Then Pharisees and scribes came to Jesus from Jerusalem and said, 'Why do your disciples transgress the tradition of the elders? For they do not wash their hands when they eat.' He answered them, 'And why do you transgress the commandment of God for the sake of your tradition? For God commanded, "Honor your father and your mother," and, "He who speaks evil of father or mother, let him surely die." But you say, "If any one tells his father or his mother, 'What you would have gained from me is given to God, he need not honor his father.' So, for the sake of your tradition, you have made void the word of God." (http://www. secondexodus.com/html/ jewishcatholicdialogue/personalqualifications. htm)

In conclusion, Jewish leaders still accuse Jesus Christ of Heresy and Blasphemy and those who support his teachings are no different.

To be called a Heretic by the Jewish leaders does not offend the author, since he is commanded by our Lord to Love our neighbor. The author encourages the Jewish leaders to Love the Lord our God with all their Heart, Mind, and Soul and may the Lord judge them with shalom. (Matthew 18:16-21)

Because no one has ever fulfilled the Bible's description of this future king, Jews still await the coming of the Messiah. Christians counter that Jesus will fulfill these in the second coming, but Jewish sources show that the

Messiah will fulfill the prophecies outright. When Jesus Christ was nailed to the cross he said, "I am thirsty." A jar of wine vinegar was there, so they soaked a sponge in it, put the sponge on a stalk of the hyssop plant, and lifted it to Jesus' lips. When he had received the drink, Jesus said, "It is finished." This means that he accomplished all that God required for the purpose of reconciliation. When Jesus rose from the dead on the third day he proved that the seeds for us to believe and follow the greatest commandment have been laid. The seed must be planted and the crop allowed to grow before it can be harvested.

Seeking God to do it all at once would be a miracle and how would the Jewish leaders judge themselves based on that miracle? It would be difficult to relate to it and thus soon be ignored.

There will be signs in the Sun, Moon and Stars. On earth, nations will be in anguish and perplexity at the roaring and tossing of the sea. Men will faint from terror, apprehensive of what is coming in a cloud with power and great glory. When these things begin to take place, stand up and lift up your heads, because your redemption is drawing near. (Luke21:25-28). Since many will be judged and many more forgiven, thus the harvest will be plentiful. He told them this parable: "Look at the fig tree and all the trees. When they sprout leaves, you can see for yourselves and know that summer is near. Even so, when you see these things happening, you know the kingdom of God is near. (Luke 21:29-31)

This is what the Kingdom of God is like. A man scatters seed on the ground. Night and Day, whether he sleeps or gets up, the seed sprouts and grows, though he does not know how. All by itself the soil produces grain first the stalk, then the head, then the full kernel in the head. As soon as the grain is ripe, he puts the sickle to it, because the harvest has come. (Mark 4:26-29) The second coming concerns the amazing harvest that has yet to come. When Jesus Christ returns the fields will be in full harvest, thus those who believe will far outnumber those who don't. Just like a field that is properly planted will produce a great harvest. The Lord will usher in an era of world peace, and end all hatred, oppression, suffering and disease. As it says: "Nation shall not lift up sword against nation, neither shall man learn war anymore." (Isaiah 2:4) The Lord will spread universal knowledge of the God of Israel, which will unite humanity as one. As it says: "God will be King over all the world—on that day, God will be One and His Name will be One" (Zechariah 14:9).

Human evolution is associated with the development of the human race from lower forms of life including fish and bacteria. Why is the virgin birth significant? God chose to bring his son to earth by virgin birth, if it was good enough for his son then it would be good enough for Adam and Eve. The virgin birth is not so rare in sharks. A zebra shark named Zebedee that lives in the restaurant aquarium in Dubai's Burj Al Arab is reproducing parthenogenetically, meaning that embryos are developing from eggs unfertilized by male sperm.

Although Zebedee's offspring are genetically very similar to her, they aren't identical clones, since her DNA is recombined during the reproductive process. When a human baby boy is conceived by sexual reproduction one chromosome from the male sperm is delivered to the egg where one chromosome from the female will unite with it to form a diploid chromosome. During the development of the boy the genes will cross over between the two original chromosomes, thus making them much more similar. Thus Jesus was not a clone of his mother neither are Virgin births of known invertebrates and a variety of vertebrates, including hammerhead, blacktip, and bamboo sharks because of gene cross over occurring before the organism becomes an adult. Since it is so common, the search is on for the gene controlling it. "Everyone's looking for it in sharks now, and I think it's always there to be found," said marine biologist Demian Chapman of Stony Brook University in New York State. "Since a very wide range of sharks can do it, I think it's reasonable to speculate that all sharks can do this." Virgin birth could be an evolutionary adaptation that allows species to squeak through tough times. For example, Chapman said, "it could give sharks a bit of an edge when colonizing new habitats—they don't necessarily have to look for males in a place they want to live. "It's not as good as finding a male, because females don't seem to produce as many offspring as compared to when they mate." As perhaps the ultimate form of inbreeding, parthenogenesis also results in offspring with low genetic diversity, and therefore greater likelihood of immune systems unable to handle a variety of threats, among other potential side effects. Even so, virgin birth "can be a way to persist in a difficult environment or when population density is low," he said. http://news.nationalgeographic. com/news/2012/01/120106-virgin-birth-shark-dubai-science/

Human evolution from lower animals as documented in natural history museums would only be possible by virgin birth of Adam and Eve in order to establish a moral and just human government. If we got all the way to Apes without the law, then why would we need it now? Why would humans need to evolve a new law, since we could easily point the finger at our Ape ancestors towards how successful they were at survival? Moreover human law is opposite of natural selection, since it is against the law for a younger male to kill an older male and take his territory as top predators do frequently. Jesus Christ's virgin birth was an evolutionary birth, because the virgin birth has been documented as a valid method of reproduction in various species and there is no mention of a virgin birth of any creature in the Genesis story of creation.

The Genesis story of creation and evolution from lower life forms are complete opposites. The goal is not to bring them together to form a unification creation story, since a virgin birth is not recorded in Genesis. When Jesus rose from the dead and appeared to the disciples, God demonstrated his power associated with miracles being the opposite of what is expected. How Jesus Christ lived makes his birth even more significant!

His birth alone is remarkable enough, since it is accountable for eukaryotes evolving from prokaryotes displayed in the virgin birth gene.

Chapter 6

Queen of the South

If you won't be better tomorrow than you were today, and then what do you need tomorrow for?

Rabbi Nahman of Bratslav

I n 1973 the United States Supreme court's decision made it possible for women to make a personal choice to have an abortion. A man can't force a woman to have an abortion. However, a woman can have an abortion without the legal consent of the father. Abortion is clearly a woman's choice. Now when the queen of Sheba heard of the fame of Solomon concerning the name of the LORD, she came to test him with hard questions. She came to Jerusalem with a very great retinue, with camels bearing spices and very much gold and precious stones. And when she came to Solomon, she told him all that was on her mind. And Solomon answered all her questions; there was nothing hidden from the king that he could not explain to her. And when the queen of Sheba had seen all the wisdom of Solomon, the house that he had built, the food of his table, the seating of his officials, and the attendance of his servants, their clothing, his cupbearers, and his burnt offerings that he offered at the house of the LORD, there was no more breath in her.—1ˢᵗ Kings 10:1-5

Then some of the scribes and Pharisees answered him, saying, "Teacher, we wish to see a sign from you." But he answered them, "An evil and adulterous generation seeks for a sign, but no sign will be given to it except the sign of the prophet Jonah. For just as Jonah was three days and three nights in the belly of the great fish, so will the Son of Man be three days and three nights in the heart of the earth. The men of Nineveh will rise up at the judgment with this generation and condemn it, for they repented at the preaching of Jonah, and behold, something greater than Jonah is here. The queen of the South will rise up at the judgment with this generation and condemn it, for she came from the ends of the earth to hear the wisdom of Solomon, and behold, something greater than Solomon is here.—Matthew 12:38-42

Why is queen of the South significant for a woman's choice to have an abortion? The queen of Sheba is referenced by Jesus, because she sought out the truth and accepted it. The Pharisees rejected the truth, because they were too interested in climbing the ladder of success to become a chief priest based upon what was already written. How does one typically behave when they get to the top of the ladder? Few Jewish religious texts have provoked as much indignation and discomfort as the brief passage that is recited by traditional Jewish men at the beginning of the daily morning prayers: "Blessed are you, Lord, our God, ruler the universe who has not created me a woman." It is found in the Talmud and meant to accompany activities that are performed in the course of waking up in the morning, such as hearing the first cock-crow, opening one's eyes, stepping on the ground, getting dressed, etc. The "has not created me a woman" blessing is part of a subgroup that expresses similar gratitude for not having been created a gentile (i.e., a heathen) or a slave.

Contemporary apologists for the blessing insist that the blessing is not intended to disparage women or imply that they are inferior, but merely to express gratitude for the fact that men are obligated to perform more religious commandments. The point here is that when one makes it to the top of the ladder, then the attitude becomes thank you for not making me like those beneath the ladder. Moreover, this is the primary reason the Pharisees rejected Jesus Christ. They cared more about the praise of men than the praise of God. The queen of the South was not afraid to ask questions, because ask and it will be given to you; seek and you will find; knock and the door will be opened to you. For anyone who asks receives; he who seeks finds; and to him who knocks, the door will be opened (Matthew 7:78). The queen of the south desired to know the truth, so that she would not make incomprehensible decisions. A woman that choses to abort her child is making an incompressible decision, because the world or Earth has displayed that it contains the meaning of life. Life on Earth is meaningless as Solomon makes clear in Ecclesiastes. The Queen of the South sought the meaning of life since women are the producer of human life as the Supreme Court in the US makes clear. The hope is that the women choosing to have an abortion will learn that God is comprehendible and create a child of God.

According to Satan there are two types of people in this world, those that build the ladder and those that climb the ladder. In 2 Corinthians 4:4 Satan, who is the god of this world, has blinded the minds of those who don't believe. They are unable to see the glorious light of the Good News. They don't understand this message about the glory of Christ, who is the exact likeness of God. Satan uses the ladder to get people of the world to follow his way. The ladder is very enticing, since it makes us appear as being needed the most. Jonah struggled with this and wanted all the people of Nineveh destroyed because he said God would destroy them because of their evil ways. The people of Nineveh believed God and did not bring upon them the destruction he had threatened. So, why did Jonah get angry with God for not destroying the Ninevites? Jonah was angry enough to die, but God relates the people of Nineveh to a vine that he did not tend or make it grow. If the more than a hundred and twenty thousand people were destroyed at Nineveh according to Jonah's anger, then Jonah's story would not have been about praying to God and seeking to do his will.

Jonah loved the holy temple and prayed to God to use him since the word of the lord came to him to go to the city of Nineveh and preach against it. When Jonah ran from the word of the Lord and headed for Tarshish the sailors cast lots and the lot fell on Jonah. The point here is that Jonah lied in his prayer to God, since worship means I will do as you ask. He states to the sailors "I am a Hebrew and I worship the Lord, the God of heaven, who made the sea and the land. Life is a game to those who desire to get to the top of the ladder. The second commandment states that we should love one another, is this possible or just a naive statement that should be dismissed as being too difficult to follow in order to get to the top of the ladder? What role does the adult have to prevent abortion? Why does this matter; is it associated with the meaning of life or how comfortable life will be in future generations? Is abortion a method the government supports mainly to control population growth, since Human population is growing like never before and inflation is associated with supply and demand of natural resources? We are now adding *one billion* people to the planet every 12 years. That's about 220,000 per day. Since there is not another planet like Earth for us to go to and live, then will the reader act like Jonah and acknowledge that God knows what he is doing or will the reader act like Satan the god of this world.

The list of problems the god of this world is causing because of greed, or at least complicating, is a long one. It includes shortages of all our resources, war and social conflict, limits on personal freedom, overcrowding and the health and survival of other species.(www.howmany.org) This is only true if the carrying capacity of the environment is limited to current technologies and human ignorance about the meaning of life. What is the purpose of the Church? Let's examine the two scenarios first and then the purpose will become clear.

1) Adults few in number and children great in number going to heaven (caused by abortion and other selfish decisions made by adults). Christ victorious, since the numbers in heaven would be greater than the numbers in Hell. Satan took one third of the angels out of heaven, thus numbers do matter.

2) Adults high in number and children low in number going to heaven (because more grow to become adults—fewer child deaths). Christ victorious, since the numbers in heaven would be greater than the numbers in Hell. The point is that Jesus is going to be victorious, and the question becomes will the church do its job and promote child to adult love of God.

Christ is victorious in both cases, so what is the point! In example number one, this is the current state of life on Earth. The large number of children going to heaven is the result of abortion, child disease from water or lack of food, and accidental death. The point is that the numbers going to heaven will always be greater than those going to Hell because of the grace of our Lord.

The goal of the Church is to establish a government based on the foundation of Jesus Christ. (Isaiah 9:6) A government established on Christ will promote child to adult love of God. This is the goal of the Church.

Death in plagues and natural disasters can be prevented, since the Holy Spirit can direct and inform those willing to listen that will promote child to adult love of God.

The Lord will not be defeated by children growing up and not loving God and establishing Hell on Earth and defeat in Heaven, thus it child to adult love of God is not promoted by the church expect more war and child death as outlined in the first scenario.

The author supports organizations that help prevent abortion, since this is the way to defeat it. Should abortion remain legal? Can we stop murder? No, murders take place even with the death penalty as a deterrent. If a person commits a crime, then executing a person for that crime does not change the fact that the person will die, it only changes the time. What the death penalty does is promote an eye for an eye, thus as a Christian I am not for it. However a role of government is to protect its citizens, thus when it chooses to execute it is reminding us of the power God has to destroy. Suicide and Abortion share similar characteristics, usually counseling can be given to encourage someone not to kill him or herself. However, he or she may still choose to kill him or herself. God gives us the free will to choose, thus choice is a gift from God. The problem here is that men do not hold women accountable very well. Women do a better job holding other women accountable for violent behavior. I believe prison time should be given to those who chose to make violent choices. To make abortion illegal would not stop it, so I support the following:

Women who chose to have an abortion without medical help would be tried for the murder of the unborn child and if found guilty would serve a minimum of 10 years in prison.

Women who chose to have a medically assisted abortion would be required by law to serve 3 years in a minimum—security prison. The point is to establish justice for a crime that occurred. Most criminals are repeat offenders, until they reconcile which results in peace. The role of government is to establish justice, because without it eventually there will be no peace. If a government supports injustice for financial reasons, then it is planning for its own financial failure.

The author is a sinner and will sin till death. Not recognizing this fact will cause the individual to show no mercy. Is the mother demonstrating mercy to the baby being aborted?

It's unfortunate that it's turned into such a personal attack on an issue that's such a personal decision," said the president of the Jefferson County and Kentucky National Organization for Women chapters.

The personal decision concerns using birth control. Birth control as defined as tools that prevent the sperm and egg from forming a zygote. Once the zygote is formed, then plans for a child have been made. Once this occurs, then the outcome must be supported. Therefore the personal decision concerns using birth control. When that personal decision is made, the outcome must be supported.

Outcome A: no child conceived.

Outcome B child conceived.

If we choose not to support outcome B, then we are establishing an oxymoron to validate murder. A baby that has not made it out of the womb would be considered a frail or weak product of life. A baby can't survive once born on its own. It must be feed it can't eat adult food. Thus a newborn baby is just as frail as a baby in the mother.

If a woman chooses to have an abortion, then she should receive punishment for the crime. Placing women in prison for prostitution or selling drugs and not for murder is an injustice. Do aborted children go to Heaven? A Bar Mitzvah or Jewish celebration of adulthood occurs between 12-13 years of age. At this time the adult understands that he or she will one day die. Most people do not want to die. However children do not comprehend death, thus they have no desire to lash out at God over this punishment. Adults that have lost children understand this point. Moreover since children do not see death as a punishment, they do not need reconciliation.

Thus unless corrupted by an adult all children go to heaven. If corrupted the adult could face spiritual destruction. Which means God would not send that spirit to hell, but destroy that spirit. How? Each spirit is a pure and distinct ratio of God himself. God can choose to change that ratio and destroy that spirit, since God has the power to create and destroy. Remember atoms are defined by ratios of protons, neutrons and electrons. The difference is that we were created to be infinite.

Truth can be understood, because it comes from Jesus Christ. A story with lies makes no sense, because Satan is the father of lies. God can be understood, however the leader of evil makes no sense. Moreover, the author supports organizations that help women keep their child, and requests that the reader do the same. Governments that worship an incomprehensible God will die by the sword because they live by the sword as an eye for an eye lacks forgiveness. The worship of an incomprehensible God does not promote child to adult love of God, therefore war is to be expected.

Chapter 7

Matthew 22:37

The Samaritan woman said to Jesus, "You are a
Jew and I am a Samaritan woman. How can you
ask me for a drink? (For Jews do not associate
with Samaritans).

John 4:9

The Samaritans were only partly Jewish, and they worshipped God
differently than the Jews of Israel. Jews from Judea and Galilee
hated the Samaritans. They would go out of their way to travel
around Samaria. Leviticus 19:18 does not define whom your neighbor is
and the reason for the following description:

Jesus, who is my neighbor?

[30] And Jesus answering said, A certain man went down from Jerusalem to
Jericho, and fell among thieves, which stripped him of his raiment, and
wounded him, and departed, leaving him half dead.

[31] And by chance there came down a certain priest that way: and when he
saw him, he passed by on the other side.

[32] And likewise a Levite, when he was at the place, came and looked on
him, and passed by on the other side.

³³ But a certain Samaritan, as he journeyed, came where he was: and when he saw him, he had compassion on him,

³⁴ And went to him, and bound up his wounds, pouring in oil and wine, and set him on his own beast, and brought him to an inn, and took care of him. (Luke 10:30-34)

This scripture states that Jesus calls us to love those who are different from us. The Catholic Church baptizes infants for the purpose of removing original sin, so they worship God differently than the protestant church. (John 4:1-2) It was not Jesus who baptized but his disciples. Peter was the first pope and Jesus states and I tell you that you are Peter, and on this rock I will build my church, and the gates of Hades will not overcome it. (Matthew 6:18) The Thirty Years' War (1618-1648) was a series of wars principally fought in Central Europe, involving most of the countries of Europe. It was one of the longest and most destructive conflicts in European history, and one of the longest continuous wars in modern history. It was fought largely as a religious war between Protestants and Catholics in the Holy Roman Empire, although disputes over internal politics and the balance of power within the Empire played a significant part. The point here is that Satan is very similar to us in that he has a spirit, so he can relate to us and cause us to follow him. When we do not love our neighbor, we desire our neighbor to be a servant and not a friend. A master seeks to control the servant and keep them from becoming knowledgeable about the chain of command. The borrower is slave to the lender.

All of the law is built on the first and second commandment. Every law that follows is meant to be methods to make following the Greatest Commandment become a desire of the heart, mind, and soul. Outwardly you look like righteous people, but inwardly your hearts are filled with hypocrisy and lawlessness. (Matthew 23:28) What sorrow awaits you teachers of religious law and you Pharisees? Hypocrites! For you cross land and sea to make one convert, and then you turn that person into twice the child of hell you yourselves are! (Matthew 23:15)

How could this be, since the Pharisee were doing the best they could to follow the law? Their worship is a farce, for they teach man-made ideas as commands from God. Why there is such a need to teach man made ideas? The goal is to establish a business, so that future clients will pay the bills. What is the difference between a witch doctor and a medical doctor?

Both are not seeking to give God credit for healing an illness. The medical doctor uses science and the witch doctor uses natural remedies handed down or learned by trial and error. The love of God concerns giving God credit; so no one can boast. The goal of the witch doctor or medical doctor is to make it known that they are the best at their profession, so that they can get more clients. A child of hell is one that seeks to climb the ladder to the top and views others as being inferior to their work.

So what happens when the top of the ladder seems out of reach? African Americans are more likely to be charged with a crime associated with marijuana than whites. Drug use is a serious epidemic in this country and has been for many decades. A drug provides the same experience and if used repetitively more is required to get the same result. A drug addict does not trust people and has turned to the drug to fill the need for love or acceptance. Loving god concerns accepting the beauty and diversity of his creation and not trying to limit it to only a few things are beautiful. (Matthew 15:9) Some Pharisees and teachers of religious law now arrived from Jerusalem to see Jesus. They asked him, "Why do your disciples disobey our age-old tradition? For they ignore our tradition of ceremonial hand washing before they eat." (Matthew 15:1-2) All of the law is built on the first and second commandment. Every law that follows is meant to be ways to make following the Greatest Commandment become a desire of the heart, mind, and soul. Laws that do not promote the following of the greatest commandment are age old traditions that need to be changed! Unfortunately many will not be saved, because they do not love God. Thus there is no desire within to accept the free gift of salvation.

Don't misunderstand why I have come. I did not come to abolish the Law of Moses or the writings of the prophets. No, I came to accomplish their purpose. (Matthew 5:17) Grace is a personal invitation to Heaven and it is offered to all who will receive it. Those who are baptized and do not change their ways and obey The Greatest Commandment will not be chosen. (Matthew 22:14) For this reason there are many false preachers, because they will argue or provide reasons why they are not capable of loving God as written in Matthew 23:28. John 3:16 states for God so loved the world that he gave his one and only son, that whoever believes in him shall not perish but have eternal life.

What does believes in Jesus Christ mean? Does it mean born of a virgin and died on the cross for our sins? No, this is what Jesus did so that you would believe his command to love one another. The Pharisee asked Jesus for a miracle, so that they could believe his command to love one another. Thus it is too easy to get lost in the miracles and not believe the command Jesus Christ gives to love one another. Choices that are made whether to sell a stock, purchase a home, or get married are all based on belief in an expected outcome.

When the rich young ruler asked Jesus what must I do to have eternal life, how did Jesus answer? Did the rich young ruler believe in Jesus? Belief is an action word as Jonah demonstrated and boasting about it is not showing that belief to be true as stated in Ephesians 2:8-9. If God tells you to do something, the mind can easily find a way to change the belief. If God tells you to do something, it is a belief because it is almost impossible to get others to believe you unless their life becomes threated as stated in Jonah1:10. A false preacher is jealous of the power Jesus Christ has before he came to Earth and after he came to offer an invitation to those who follow Deuteronomy 6:5. Thus they are not chosen and will not be in Heaven. Grace is not above The Greatest Commandment; Grace is the primary reason for a Christian to follow Matthew 22:37. A false preacher is a control freak, since the subconscious desire to be seen as a main part of the chain of command prevents thy kingdom come thy will be done on Earth as it is in Heaven.

God desires to have a relationship with us through the power of the Holy Spirit. The love of money makes this impossible to accomplish, the devil knows this and promotes it by getting us to believe what others think of us really matters. Fame . . . One day the Earth will be engulfed by the Sun and all that we have done will be gone. No evidence will exist that we were ever on this Earth. No one to believe or carry on to the next generation anything you said was true. (Luke 4:5-7) Jesus clearly understands that Earth was not created as an eternal place. Therefore love of money is a false illusion of eternal remembrance.

God gives us talents that are unique. What does Adam and Eve were created in the image of God mean? Adam and Eve desired more, they were not content with being created in the image of God; they understood the difference between what is good and evil, since they were created in the image of God. However they wanted more (Eve wanted more of the talents Adam was given and she instructed Adam that he would be better if he took without permission from the tree) and they chose to steal from the tree of the knowledge of good and evil. Adam and Eve were not content with what God had given them, since perfection was not enough and they wanted more. How could perfection not be enough? The fall occurred after Eve was created out of Adam. Adam and Eve were very different from each other and God gives us talents that are unique as well. Jealousy over the perfect gifts that God gave Adam and Eve led to the desire for more which was disrespectful to God; thus the fall of Adam and Eve is a warning to us not to tell God what to do or what is best. Many see God as being different before Jesus came and died on the cross, thus the Old and New Testament. This is a false conclusion, God is the same and his law is the same. (Matthew 5:17) Matthew 5:17 means Christians are still accountable to the law. Being saved by grace concerns Christ's forgiveness of your sin and should give you more reason to follow The Greatest Commandment. What more could God give you to make you desire to follow his law? Being saved by grace is a gift from God. The ungrateful are not chosen, since they have no desire to change their ways and love God as Jesus instructed the rich young ruler. Anyone attempting to place a law above The Greatest Commandment is no different than Adam and Eve trying to tell God what is best.

Did Jesus come to abolish the law or fulfill it? If Christianity is the only way to heaven, then he came to abolish the law. Christianity being the only way would be the new law (saved by grace is all it takes). Unfortunately, John 3:16 is not fully being explained since it states whomever believes in me will not perish. To believe in Christ means you agree with what he says and act upon it as stated in James 2:14-26. It you have no idea what Jesus says, then how can you believe in him? Just to accept the name Jesus with no belief in him leads to the quote from Mahatma Gandhi, "I like your Christ, I do not like your Christians. Your Christians are so unlike your Christ".

The law associated with Christianity and the reason for the church concerns preparing the way for the return of our Lord. As a Christian, it is important to understand your purpose. How can we be certain that the person with the wrong cloths at the wedding banquet is analogous to The Greatest Commandment? Could anything else represent the cloths? No, anything else or any other law would be trumped or miss the mark compared to The Greatest Commandment.

If we examine the parable of the wedding banquet, some important conclusions can be reached. If you were invited to a wedding and were enjoying the good food and company and someone asked you to leave, you would most likely try to negotiate a way to remain at the party. However, the one wearing the wrong cloths says nothing when confronted and is removed from the party. Anything said would not have mattered because of John 5:41-42. This says that if you do not have the love of God in your heart, then your opinion means nothing to Jesus Christ. How do we know Jesus was talking about the greatest commandment in the parable of the wedding banquet? The guest wearing the wrong cloths did not try to negotiate.

Once saved always saved? Is Christianity the only way to Heaven? The purpose of this chapter is to acknowledge Jesus Christ as the strongest link in the heavenly chain of command, since he has the power to make an offering to those who follow the Greatest Commandment and the power to offer that authority to those who accept his Holy Spirit. (Matthew 22:14) He is the strongest link in the Heavenly circular chain of command, since he was able to leave heaven knowing he would return to heaven in the same state that he left it. In a linear chain of command when the master leaves, then those left in charge will seek to become the new leader. If this happens on Earth, war can result associated with the division of whom should be the new leader.

If I am a good Jew, good Muslim, or good person will I go to Heaven? The first commandment is the greatest commandment, because it determines whether a Non-Christian receives an offering to Heaven and whether a Christian remains in Heaven. This should be of no surprise, when members of a club don't follow the rules they are asked to leave. They might say, "We use to belong to that club". To say that they were never apart of the club would be a false statement.

"Where we come from", a poem based on "Homeland" a true account of a Hungarian survivor of the Holocaust by Lois E. Olena.

> It was Christmas eve so the Arrow Cross took the children,
> out to the Danube
> and filled their little bellies with bullets
> flipping them
> into the congealing, icy river below.
> It was the Red Danube
> that night,
> choking on the blood
> of orphan Jews.

Psalm 137

⁵If I forget thee, O Jerusalem, let my right hand forget her cunning.

⁶If I do not remember thee, let my tongue cleave to the roof of my mouth; if I prefer not Jerusalem above my chief joy.

Poems like this show that even in the worst of times, many still chose to love the Lord our God with all their Heart, Mind, and Soul. Jesus Christ is the only way to Heaven; the Lord is not limited by Christianity! Those who love God obey the greatest commandment by loving all that is good, and will receive grace. The Lord can do whatever he wants to do; immeasurably more which is why he is the King of Heaven. If I am a good Muslim or good Jew and I die, then the Lord may choose to give me an offering John 5:25 (Verily, verily, I say unto you, The hour is coming, and now is, when the dead shall hear the voice of the Son of God: and they that hear shall live). If I am a good Jew, Muslim, or person, then when I die and the Lord chooses to give me an offering what made me good? How could I be chosen while others perished in Hell? Moses provides the answer to this question. Moses was not sinless, however if you are Jewish when you die you will be judged by Moses John 5:45-46 ("But do not think I, Jesus Christ will accuse you before the Father. Your accuser is Moses, on whom your hopes are set. If you believed Moses, you would believe me,). Moses is judge of the Jewish Nation, so what is Moses looking for in order for him to give an offering into heaven by the authority of our Lord and Savior Jesus Christ? If I am a good Jew, I can get into Heaven by the forgivness of Moses based on the authority of Jesus Christ through the nature of the heavenly circular chain of command.

Does being a good person really matter? Any good Jew would say yes! What makes a good Jew? When a good Jew dies, what is Moses looking for in the description of a good Jew? Moses is looking for one characteristic; do you have the LOVE of GOD in your Heart? A good Jew does well, because he or she has the Love of God in his or her Heart. This is what makes a Muslim good and a person good. If you are a Jew, Muslim, or person and are judged not to have the love of god in your heart, then you will not be given access to Heaven!

Am I a follower or a leader? In the Universe, in order to be a leader I must be the absolute best at what I do or I am just a follower of the one who is the best. This is the point of Jesus, he is good. He is the leader of good. If you think you are good, then you will be put to the test and others will see your faults and point them out to you. If you think you are the father of evil, then you will soon see that you were just a follower and that the leader of evil existed long before your creation.

We can talk all day about what is good, however evil is clearly evident. Torture . . . Murder . . . Rape . . . Good has nothing to do with any of that latter. Why is Jesus Christ the only way to God? For many, implying that there is only one way to God is restrictive. In order to answer the first question, we must look at one accomplishment that Christ had that no other person has achieved. Christ is the only way to God, because he is the only one who has ever defeated Satan. Let's say hypothetically, I am playing a video game. The objective of the game is to defeat the opponent to win. This may sound easy, but to defeat your opponent might be extremely difficult. Many could play this game for years and never win. Once someone won the game everyone would want to know THE WAY. Thus the only way to get to heaven is to defeat the one that is trying to take you to hell. Satan desires you to believe in him and follow his behavior to achieve Earthly success in the form of wealth or power. Jesus Christ is the only way to God, because he is the only way to defeat Satan or Evil by not following his plan on Earth. Thus every human being that has been on this planet has either faced judgment through Satan or forgiveness through Jesus Christ. Judgment always holds on to the memory of sin. The beauty of the forgiveness that Jesus gives removes the sin as if it never happened. This is called freedom from sin.

If I am Muslim, and the Lord knows that I have the Love of God in my Heart why would I convert to Christianity? No need. If you are not a Christian and you die, then you will be judged! The Lord will judge you and determine whether you have the Love of God in your heart. This may anger many Christians; however Christianity is not the only way to God. Christians are of many denominations based on issues like once saved always saved. When a person is baptized they are saved, to question the salvation is to question the baptism. Do not question the baptism; otherwise any sin committed by the best of persons could bring salvation into question. Once a person is baptized, then their sins are forgiven. When they die they will face forgiveness and be granted access to Heaven. This tends to upset a good Jew. Why be good, if all I have to do is get baptized?

Jesus spoke of this issue in the parable of the wedding banquet. Christianity offers an invitation to all. However some that get in are not wearing the correct cloths and are thrown out. Wearing the correct cloths concerns the love of God in your heart, mind, and soul; it is the greatest commandment. Jesus is not the ticket for getting away with not loving all that is good. Jesus replied, "'you must love the Lord your God with all your heart, all your soul, and your entire mind. This is the first and greatest commandment.

Moses was not sinless nor baptized, however he is in heaven and judging the Jewish Nation. The "correct cloths" is one issue and it is an important issue. Many Christians get into Heaven and are thrown out because they do not have the love of God in their heart, mind and soul. They were saved and received forgiveness, however Heaven is a Kingdom and Christ will not be fooled by a follower who does not obey the greatest commandment. (Matthew 22:14)

All of the law is built on the first and second commandment. Every law that follows is meant to be ways to make following the Greatest Commandment become a desire of the heart, mind, and soul. Laws that do not promote the following of the greatest commandment are age old traditions that need to be changed!!! 1 Corinthians 15:29 would be a New Testament example.

Some Christians view Mormons as being part of a cult; since Mormons baptize the dead which demonstrates they believe that GRACE is not a choice. However if a Christian says they are saved by Grace and not by works, then they are subconsciously agreeing with the Mormons that Grace is not a choice 1 Corinthians 15:29. The point here is that God does not require us to be good, He does require us to Love all that is good. It is a choice to love all that is good, thus to get into heaven one will be chosen by our Lord. The statement "Saved by Grace" has led many to believe that the choices they make do not matter. The fulfillment of the Law is associated with showing us that God is good. Jesus clearly stated that he was God in the flesh, thus God only has good intentions. Therefore, what else could God give you to make you desire to follow his law or to Love him? The question is why does Evil have the power to control Earthly wealth? Jesus was tempted with Earthly wealth by the devil, and in that temptation the devil makes it clear what he wants.

Job was a man of great wealth; however he gained that wealth without a love for money. Since money can make one look better or appear to have chosen to sin less than those with fewer material possessions. **One sin is all it took for Satan to be thrown out of Heaven.** The rich man in the

New Testament had a love for money similar to the parable of the man whom builds multiple storage bins for the excess crops harvested and the next day he died. The love of money is associated with personal control over your own destiny or the freedom to do what you want; thus hoarding results, because work is never easy as Job would attest. If work were so easy, then why do the rich hoard money? 1%? Those who hoard money fear that they may have to do work other than what they desire. Luke 16:13 (NIV) "No servant can serve two masters. Either he will hate the one and love the other, or he will be devoted to the one and despise the other. You cannot serve both God and Money." Job did not fear work, he embraced it.

Is God only good? John 10:34-38, When Jesus says I and the father are one; he is displaying the behavior of God. This upset the religious leaders, so Jesus quoted (Psalm 82:6) If you want to understand the people of the Old Testament and their passion for Moses and Elijah, then read this psalm. Did Noah do everything that God asked? (Genesis 6:18, Genesis 7:1) How many times did God ask Jonah to do his will? The story of Jonah is real, since it is the reason Jesus waits 3 days to rise from the grave. (Matthew 12:38-40) Moreover, if you ask most religious scholars why the world is corrupt they will say because of the fall of Adam and Eve. Adam and eve are to blame!!! The chosen in heaven don't blame Adam and Eve, since Jesus accepted blame for all sin. Chosen because grace is a choice. The devil has no dominion in heaven and can't be blamed in heaven for the choices we made on Earth, because of free will. Why? Jesus Christ is a representation of how good is stronger than evil, since good can support any burden that evil can bring to bear. The point here is that God does not require us to be good, He does require us to Love all that is good. Unfortunately many have no desire within to accept the free gift of salvation, thus they will not be saved from judgment.

Chapter 8

John the Baptist

Life without a friend is death without a witness.

Spanish proverb

The objective of this chapter is to provide reasons why Jesus is the sacrifice needed for our reconciliation with God; also a call to prepare the way for the return of Jesus Christ like John the Baptist prepared the way for his death, burial, and resurrection. When we are baptized our sins are forgiven by Jesus Christ. We become born again. Since our sins are forgiven we become sinless, however this does not mean we will not sin again. We can fall again just like Adam and Eve. It is still important that we repent and ask Christ for forgiveness of a sinful act. Lastly, when we repent and confess our sins to God we are seeking his forgiveness. (Matthew 3:2-6) Could there be unity in Heaven between those who do not love God and those who do? (John 5:41-42) Those who do not love God are not willing to follow those who love the law, thus chaos would result between both in heaven. Baptism is not a free ticket to get out of following The Greatest Commandment. Jesus did not tell the rich young ruler to go and be baptized when he asked Jesus," What must I do to obtain eternal life". John 3:16 states For God so loved the world that he gave his one and only Son, that whoever believes in him shall not perish but have eternal life. The point to this scripture concerns believes in him. This means the words Christ states. Those words require work to believe and that is the reason the rich young ruler could not accept the words of Jesus Christ.

John the Baptist was the wisest man that ever lived, since he is the best example of how to follow the leader of love. If we look at the church, in order to baptize someone you must first be baptized since the gift of the Holy Spirit is associated with Baptism! Believing this results in the forgiveness of sin and peace. There is no record of anyone baptizing John before he started baptizing for the forgiveness of sin. Scriptures make this point, even Christ pointed this out. When Jesus was Baptized by John the Baptist he (John the Baptist) received forgiveness of sin., which is even more evidence that John the Baptist was the greatest man that ever lived aside from Jesus. How do we know that John was Baptized or received forgiveness of sin when he baptized Jesus. Jesus did not need to be forgiven of any sin. What sin was Jesus forgiving John? Most likely the inherited sin from Adam and Eve; John the Baptist was not perfect and as scriptures state he did not have the power to forgive sin and he did not forgive the sin of Herod. Jesus could have just told John the Baptist that his sins were forgiven. However, Jesus humbled himself and allowed John to have great honor when he (John the Baptist) was baptized (John the Baptists sins were forgiven) for the forgiveness of sin. If neither John nor Jesus needed to be Baptized, then that event was meaningless. When we say that Jesus became sin, we are acknowledging that he took on our sin or accepted blame for it and was punished on the Cross for them. Why would he do that? The answer is love, since God knows that we could not handle the punishment required for our sin.

John the Baptist was given the authority to Baptize from Heaven. This is important to recognize, since John Baptized many prior to his own Baptism. At church only those that have been Baptized, Baptize new believers. It is like the leader and the follower. However, the Baptism of John the Baptist is unique. Why? John the Baptist was a sinner and Jesus was not. So as a sinner and Baptizing one who is without sin what does that make John the Baptist? It made him sinless. John the Baptist is the best example of a Jesus Christ follower. Moreover, Jesus gave John the authority to receive his Baptism in a most honorable way. Similar to one who gets a PHD without the credit hours, but the work to show it was deserved. In this Baptism of John the Baptist, does Jesus look like a King who should be served or a King who is a servant?

Do I desire to follow John the Baptist? Why do I ask? John the Baptist ministered to the homeless. He ate bugs with honey. I live in a home, so if I behaved like John the Baptist my neighbors would not relate to me. Thus should the reader drink alcohol, since many do not because of John the Baptist as Luke 7:33 states? For some two drinks of alcohol a day promotes good health, and for others it does not promote good health. Some people are allergic to peanuts, thus in the same way alcohol may not be good for their health. The author gets a cold or the flu more often when alcohol is consumed. The author would not refuse a drink in order to promote the gospel to a neighbor, however the author understands that sacrifice is sometimes necessary to get the attention of the lost. It is important to observe what makes your body healthy, since it needs to be strong and ready to pick up the cross when Christ calls for your help. The weak always turn the other way, since their need for enjoyment outweighs the discipline needed to maintain a healthy lifestyle. The point is that John the Baptist took risks preparing the way. He could relate to those around him, and he drew a large following. I encourage you to reach out to those around you and take risks to show them how much God loves them. There are only two commandments that all the law are based on which we must follow. How does following Jesus make you a servant? If you can't do something on your own and you ask for their help, then you are a servant. If you can do the task on your own and you still choose to serve others, then that is called LOVE. Jesus is the best example of Love; he is the leader of Love. Freedom from sin promotes peace and brings glory to God and his creation.

If Jesus had baptized John, then every baptism that John accomplished prior to his own baptism would have been declared invalid. Baptism concerns receiving the gift of the Holy Spirit to prepare the way for our Lord and Savior Jesus Christ, since when a farmer plants a seed a bountiful harvest does not take place unless the farmer tends to the needs of the crop. If you do not understand, start a garden and ignore it all summer and the following year repeat and care for the garden all summer. A difference in the quality and quantity of fruit will be observed. If a Christian does nothing with the talents he or she is given, then they will not yield fruit for the harvest.

Baptism occurs for the forgiveness of sin. If you ask most religious scholars why the world is corrupt they will say because of the fall of Adam and Eve. Adam and eve are to blame!!! The chosen in heaven don't blame Adam and Eve, since Jesus accepted blame for all sin. The devil has no dominion in heaven and can't be blamed in heaven for the choices we made on Earth, because of free will. Why? Jesus Christ is a representation of how good is stronger than evil, since good can support any burden that evil can bring to bear, for example what did Judas do when he was to blame for giving Jesus over to be crucified? Judas Iscariot could not handle the sin that he was blamed for and he killed himself, spiritual destruction follows the same path. Very often in life our sin is exposed and the grief is overwhelming and forgiveness seems out of reach. Adam and Eve being blamed for an eternity for their sin would result in their spiritual destruction. Can you imagine if every soul going to Heaven lashed out at Adam and Eve over the decision they made concerning the fall. Eventually they would be overwhelmed and seek spiritual destruction. Sin often makes one feel as though they would be better off dead or having never been born. This is the reason Jesus Christ chose to do what he did, there was no other way.

The Holy Trinity is composed of the Father, Son, and Holy Spirit. When a new believer is baptized, they receive the gift of the Holy Spirit. The kingdom of Heaven is within us in the form of a Trinity. The Heart is a representation of the passion God has for creation. The Heart has power over the Mind and the Soul. The Heart has the power to clear the Mind and ignore the Soul. The Mind is a reflection of the Son, since it is the decision maker. The Soul is led by the Holy Spirit. The Soul will lead the Mind to thoughts of success or how to accomplish a task. The Soul can be attacked by the Devil and experience thoughts of failure. This is where understanding the power of the Heart can save the believer much grief.

Spend some time getting to know the three parts that make up the whole of the Trinity within the kingdom of Heaven. The Trinity within is a reflection of the Holy Trinity in creation.

Why should families trust in God or worship God? God is one that can neither be created nor destroyed. Therefore God can't be stopped or changed. We worship a God that will never die or change. God is infinite in the Universe. God is perfect, since he can create infinite and finite forms of matter out of nothing. His mere change in movement can produce a different product. What God can do is amazing and should be glorified! Can God be proven to exist? Yes. Moses was the first to use miracles to prove the existence of God to a large group of people in Egypt. The Pharaoh believed that his gods would protect his people. Jesus spoke of those who needed miracles to believe in God, he called them a cruel and ruthless generation. Even in America preachers need miracles to prove that God exists, since they have said "that God can't be proven to exist". Moses was the first chosen by God to provide miracles to the masses to prove the existence of God our Creator. This is why the Pharisees asked Jesus to perform a sign. And he responded a wicked and adulterous generation looks for a miraculous sign. (Matthew 16:2-4) Why is this? Those who need miracles to believe in God are too caught up in their own ministry. Life is a sermon for others to see and hear the Love you have for God. The point is that God was proven to exist by Moses and the people said, "We need more miracles to believe", for example the golden calf that the Jews made when Moses went to be with God. This was after the many necessary miracles that were given to get them out of slavery in Egypt. When we associate ourselves with likeminded and those with similar behavior, then we can more easily build a big church or golden calf and encourage others to act like us. The rich man struggled with this path and it lead him to choose to follow the unforgivable sin, because he could never accept himself as being seen as financially equal to the gentiles or another similar race of people.

God can be proven to exist, the question is do you believe the miracles in the Bible? Miracles require belief, since a miracle is defined as an unusual happening, one that goes against the normal laws of nature. Can miracles be tested? If no, then this is the reason one must believe in them even when they happen right in front of your eyes.

The story of the rich man in the Bible helps us understand what the Pharisee looked like during the time of Jesus. They were really good people, better than me. Their problem was that they could not see their own small sins as significant. It only took one sin for Satan to be thrown out of Heaven. A human could easily argue that murder is worse than not loving God. This is true today of many Christians, they choose to be seen as pure and point out the major problems of others. A drop of sewage in a glass of water will make it unfit to drink. This contaminated drinking water is no better than a full glass of sewage water, since both are unfit to drink. The more a believer walks with Christ, the more the believer will learn to appreciate him; the more crowns the believer may lay at Christ's feet during his or her heavenly judgment. Would you go to a birthday party or wedding without a gift?

A true Christian will deny himself or herself like Christ did when tempted by the Devil. The devil desired to give Christ power and authority if he had chosen to bow down and be like the prideful deceiver. (Matthew 4:1-9) What does this mean to deny himself? A true believer does not concern himself or herself with self-promotion or titles. This is what John 3:16 means. Do you think the rich young ruler was a believer in Jesus Christ?

Why? Heaven is a place of unity. Christ said that whoever does the will of my father in heaven is my Brother, Sister, and Mother. In Heaven there are many different roles, however one is not seen as better than another. Christ said why you call me good only God is good. This is the point of heaven. Jesus is nothing like Satan and Christians need to remember this and take it to heart, so that they know who they serve. Many are serving the devil and don't even know it because they surround themselves with likeminded Pharisee that constantly point out problems and rarely take action to help fix them.

Truth is an important part of a family, since education concerns seeking the truth. Where does truth come from? If a person solved a difficult problem that others could not figure out, therefore he or she would be considered a genius of some sort. Did the genius invent the truth, the truth that solved a problem? A person would have to reveal himself as infinite in nature to provide evidence as the source of truth. Why? God is infinite in the Universe. God makes the truth. When the spirit listens, it may here the truth. What is true today will be true tomorrow! If you produced a truth, then you would be a God. Greek mythology provides evidence of this point. The spirit is a pure product of God. The spirit is made to be infinite, unlike atoms which change or decay into new atoms. God can create both finite and infinite products. Thus the creative power of God produces a new spirit at every human conception. God is in control. Jesus is the son of God, and what does that imply? Since God created everything, why can't I pick up a shoe and talk to God? I mean talking to a shoe as if I were talking directly to God. Also, how could I explain to my agnostic neighbor that the burning bush relates to me; thus understands me? Jesus being the Son of God implies that God communicates back to us through Jesus by the power of his holy spirit. We are human, thus we can relate to a human and not a shoe. Jesus is not more powerful than God; he is how God chose to communicate with us. We have no excuse to God when we chose not to listen to what he has to say, since he clearly has created one who is capable of listening to and relating to what we have to say.

Can God be proven to exist? Yes, the Bible gives many accounts of miracles that were witnessed by many people. Jesus, King of Heaven came to Earth in the flesh. To be God in the flesh, Jesus must understand everything. Jesus understood that God created man with free will, thus when asked when the world was going to end he said, "I don't know." (Mark 13:32) Which is the correct answer based on free will. The choices we make will determine our fate. I am not predestined to accept or reject Jesus Christ. If predestination were true, then Jesus would have given the exact date of his return. Did Christ have the power to heal himself as he was going through the crucifixion? If yes, then one could question whether he suffered. When Christ said, "My God why have you forsaken me" he left no doubt that he truly suffered.

Good, just like evil has its source. When we choose to do evil, we are reflecting that source. When we choose to do well, then we are reflecting that source. We were created with free will that is, we can choose to do as we please. However, the sources of good and evil existed before our creation. If good and evil did not exist before our creation, then predestination would be the outcome. If predestination is true, then we can't put people in prison for their choices, since they were predestined to make evil choices. Thus convicts would not be capable of being reformed with the promise of future release from prison for good behavior. Our justice system provides evidence that good and evil existed before our creation.

Earth is a part of the creation of God, so why don't we all recognize God here on Earth? Free will is the answer to this question. On earth, we have the free will to as we please. If we reflect evil, then a creation of God is shown as an imperfection. A goal of evil is to convince something that it is more perfect than something else, even though both products are made of the same essential building blocks. This may not seem like a big deal, however it is the foundation of racism from which evil flows. Satan is a creation of God. God did not make evil. Satan chose to view his building blocks as better than anything else that God had created. And seeing himself as being so good, Satan over stepped his boundaries when he tried to tell God what to do. This is the reason Satan can't be reconciled with to gain forgiveness. How can two parties reach an agreement when one will not make any concessions? Even when Jesus Christ was about to be crucified he said, "Father not my will be done". Satan has no desire to do the will of God, so his behavior is a reflection of his own choice and the reason his punishment consists of being isolated from the Kingdom of Heaven. Satan hates free will; he desires to tell you exactly what to do and if it were up to him only Hell would exist.

We desire to be remembered at our best. God created heaven first, and when Satan chose to do his will, he was thrown out of heaven. If a creation of God is not in Heaven and not on Earth, then it is in Hell. The Bible speaks of the Day of Judgment for those who have fallen. Don't be discouraged by this, since it could easily be concluded that the numbers in Hell would be greater than the numbers in Heaven. If this were the case, then Jesus Christ would not have been VICTORIOUS at Calvary.

Numbers are important; therefore because of what Christ did on the cross those in Heaven will forever more outnumber those in Hell. Jesus Christ is responsible for the victory in the battle for the Angels and Spirits over the choice between Heaven and Hell. Since it is not by works that we are saved, those that have fallen are not capable of the works required to defeat Satan. Those that have fallen are not good enough, since perfection is the requirement of Heaven. Only those Angels and spirits that choose to obey the authority of God concerning his commands will see what is good. It is by our faith in Christ; he is the only one that has been a true reflection of the fruits of the spirit, which God describes as good. Free will provides the choice to obey. The question is who are you going to obey?

In the Bible, Jesus spoke of false preachers. How do we know when we see one? The warning is meant for those doing the preaching. Does one who works more deserve more? If a preacher is doing work for himself, then he or she is concerned about heavenly rewards. If he or she goes into heaven thinking they should be served for their service, then this would be an example of a false teacher. Neither the preacher nor the student earned their way into heaven; this attitude produces disunity in Heaven. Christ said whoever does the will of the Father is his Mother, Brother, and Sister. If one enters heaven without the love of God in their Heart, Mind, and Soul, then he or she will be thrown out. How could this be possible? If all you have to do is accept Jesus Christ to get into heaven, then that opens the door to the possibility of people getting in with the wrong fruits of the spirit. It is much more difficult to serve others in Jesus name, since the money is not based on a tithe do to the fact that it requires more time. Jesus is continuing to serve today through the gift of his holy spirit.

Children are born with an innate nature to break the Ten Commandments. What does this mean? We are born without the ability to visually see Heaven. If you could see Heaven, your actions on Earth would be different. Since we can't see Heaven many don't believe it exists, so they get caught up in this world. Lacking the ability to see heaven gives us the innate nature to break the Ten Commandments. Death is the evidence for our inability to see heaven. When someone dies we can't talk to them anymore. This world will not last forever, however our lack of vision prevents us from seeing the eminent doom it faces. So why are the strong so selfish? This concerns us being spoiled and unresponsive to any help or gifts that have been given. Children can become very selfish, if they are given everything they want. If we could see Heaven, we could take everything we want. Thus, this spiritual characteristic is passed on from parents to child. If a person is mentally ill and does not know the difference between right and wrong and commits a crime we prosecute them under the insanity plea. An insane person cannot comprehend death. The fall of Adam and Eve is the reason some are born insane or become that way by drug abuse or similar action.

Sin concerns knowing the difference between right and wrong and making the wrong choice. This spiritual characteristic is passed on from our parents. Why is it impossible for humans to evolve from Bacteria or Apes? In a court of law if I know the difference between right and wrong I cannot blame someone who is insane for my crime. We cannot blame Apes or Bacteria for our crimes. If Evolution is ever made a Law, then every person that is in prison can legally declare a mistrial. Convicts are convicted on a pretense that they are a descendent of Adam and Eve as described in the Creation Story. If this story is proven false, then we have convicted the criminal under a false pretext. The foundation of our government does matter in order to establish a just and moral society. The origin of man was a distinct event and democracy is the evidence.

The best evidence for this concerns sexual molestation of children. If we evolved from Apes or Bacteria, then the man or woman that sexually molests a child can blame the child for the crime. Evolution from Apes would mean that we came from a child (Ape DNA mutation producing human child), Creation states that we came from Adam and Eve who were created as adults. Our origin is the most important part of understanding human behavior. A government under evolution does not distinguish between a child and an Adult, since it is only concerned with the Survival of the Strongest. Jesus spoke very harshly about people that sexually abuse children. He said it would have been better if they had not been born. This is the proof that evolution directly from Apes or Bacteria is incomprehensible. Something that knows the difference between right and wrong cannot blame something that does not. Jesus said," I am the way, the truth, and the life." For unto us a child is born, to us a son is given, and the government will be on his shoulders. (Isaiah9:6) Jesus turned water into wine, which is a spontaneous generation.

The creation of Adam and Eve from dust and a rib is truth, since God demonstrates to us the power of miracles and how those opposites will be on display when Jesus Christ returns. Jesus Christ did not come to disprove the Genesis story of Creation, as the Jewish leaders conclude. Jesus proved that with God anything is possible according to his divine law. Moreover, the government currently rests on the shoulders of the Torah account of our Creation. Our origin was a distinct event, an event that can only be described as a miracle. Therefore, our origin is a legal issue more than a science issue based on the Laws that say what is permissible.

Christ was not calling his persecutors insane when he said, "Father, forgive them, for they do not know what they are doing". Christ was exposing the very nature of Satan in this prayer. Christ's persecutors were totally confused, since they doubted that his birth was good enough to be Messiah. The fundamental product of doubt is confusion. Confusion is a tool Satan uses to defeat his competition. Why would Satan want to defeat his competition? Satan above all wants to be worshiped the MOST. Satan wants you to worship him as God's greatest creation. Satan knows that God can destroy him, and God knows that something would only take his place. Have you ever heard the devil you know is better than the devil you don't. More are drawn to Christ or Love than to Satan or evil.

Step one in Satan's game is to foster doubt. He did this with Judas. He planted the seed of doubt that Jesus Christ was not the messiah. Judas desired personal wealth and prestige which were not being met. So, he did what he had to do. Confused he killed himself. What other animal on Earth will make a plan to kill itself? Since most people who kill themselves do so when no one else is around to stop them, therefore suicide is most often a planned event. Satan's game concerns who should be worshiped the most. Satan is the Father of ruthlessness. Can the son be any more ruthless than the father? Satan does not want those who seek self glorification to see this, since Satan knows that with his game he is the predetermined victor. Pride goes before the fall, since the fall from personal gain is never predicted and surprisingly unexpected.

On Earth, my faith in Christ is what I lean on for my understanding of Heaven. Earthly death produces doubt of eternal control. The punishment of death for many is too great for the sin they commit, so they run around lost and declare that God does not exist. God understands that death is a harsh punishment, and for this reason he chose to reconcile with us. As a parent, when a child does something wrong and they receive punishment a similar response occurs. The child waits to see if the parent will reconcile. Reconciliation is the parents way of saying that they still love the child and long for them to be a part of the family, so they need to obey and follow the rules to prevent further punishment from occurring. Without reconciliation the further punishment for our continued sin would be Hell. Death is a harsh punishment, thus reconciliation is what Christ gave us in the hope that we would see how much God loves us.

Blessed is he who comes in the name of the Lord. This means Christ is willing to glorify those who believe in him. Christ cares about you and will listen to your needs. Christ wants you to experience unification with God. Jesus Christ denied himself personal glorification on Earth when he was tempted by the devil, so that we could see that he desires to remember us and share his love with us, otherwise we would have expected him to be out of reach. This is why Jesus Christ is Lord and the Son of God; pure love. The Son of God has reunited us with the Father. Moreover in truth there is no doubt, thus the product of truth is the absence of confusion. Christ's persecutors were totally confused, since they doubted that his birth was good enough to be Messiah.

What is Love? Do you have a little Love or a lot of Love? Love is the desire that causes most to do things that they would not normally do. Love is powerful because it makes us understand when we have it. How do we know when we have it? When you become an adult and your mom cooks you dinner without your help that would be love. Even greater Love concerns serving those who are not capable of helping accomplish the task.

Why does Jesus love you? Jesus will tell you the many reasons why he loves you. When we pray to God, we are showing God how much we love him. Who has ever given to God that God should repay him? (Romans 11:35) Jesus worshiped God like we should. Saying, Father, if thou be willing, remove this cup from me: nevertheless not my will, but thine, be done. (Luke 22:42)

How much does Jesus love you? He loves you enough to describe the kingdom of God many times to his followers; enough to show us that what he spoke about the kingdom of God is true and that life exists after death. In life many have spoken about heaven and talked about seeing light in a tunnel, but the resurrection was seen by over 500 people. This is credible evidence that Jesus is God's tool to reconcile with us over the punishment of death.

Many scoff at this idea of death being a punishment. However, not knowing what lies beyond is what death is all about. Jewish people understand this concept well, since they follow the law in the Old Testament. The law is meant to be followed, because sin produces ignorance. The more we sin the less we understand, thus a life with no restraint to sin produces a moron. My understanding of Heaven or the Kingdom of God rests with Jesus. Why? My sinful nature prevents me from understanding what lies beyond. Death is a harsh reality.

Why did Jesus choose to do the will of the Father and become sin and suffer death? Jesus loves God and he was sent to reconcile with all people not just a few. Jesus made a choice, since he could have left the earth after describing the kingdom of God to his followers. However, he did not choose to do his will! How would he have left the earth? In the same way that he is coming again.

Apathy is a lack of concern for the truth. Which basically means the truth does not matter, because death is absolute. This is why it is said, the wages of sin is death". We chose to sin over our lack of concern for the truth. Death produces a lot of anguish. The pain of dealing with this punishment over and over again throughout life can produce more apathy. Since we are a creation of God, therefore the resurrection of Jesus is God's way to reconcile with us by showing that we were created for an eternal purpose. Fundamentally, we need to know that we matter and that we will be remembered. Moreover, the resurrection is the evidence for these fundamentals.

For John Harris, saving a life and delaying its end is one and the same. Using this logic, Harris, a bioethicist at the University of Manchester in England, figures that scientists have a moral duty to extend the human life span as far as it will go, even if it means creating beings that live forever. (http://www.foxnews.com/story/0,2933,196642,00.html) John Harris knows that it has been proven that the Telomere helps determine the life span of the cell. The telomere is located on the tips of the chromosomes;

when chromosomes divide some "dummy DNA" falls off. The DNA that falls off is meant to protect the other genes from being damaged.

Who cares about this? Understanding that it is remotely possible for someone to live indefinite in the flesh validates the word of Jesus Christ. Let's imagine that you are a great real estate owner. In the course of building your wealth, a few transactions were made that caused you to lie to make the deal more profitable. When the government found out about it, they required you to sacrifice some of your belongings.

During the time of the Old Testament a sacrifice was not taken lightly. A true sacrifice meant giving up at least one of your most valuable possessions. For example, Abraham almost took Isaac as a sacrifice for his sinful behavior. A true sacrifice is meant to be a constant reminder of our previous behavior, so that we don't repeat it in the future.

A sacrifice for sinful behavior must occur or there would be no reason for people to change their ways. Therefore, knowing that Jesus Christ could have lived indefinitely in the flesh helps us as we grow in your relationship with Christ; understand how much we are missing. What do I mean how much we are missing? Do you doubt that your friendship with Christ would be stronger if Christ lived in the flesh in your house? The more I grow in Christ, the more I miss him in the flesh.

Chapter 9

The Lord's Prayer

For God is not a God of disorder but of peace—as
in all the congregations of the Lord's people.

1 Corinthians14:33

In school, when a teacher assigns homework and no one does it what happens? Students make up answers on the test. If the Lord's Prayer is the way Jesus desires us to pray, then what answers are being made up concerning the return of Jesus, what is to be expected before his return, and how should we observe the Earth prior to his return? Is Earth more like heaven or hell? The following is a comparison of Christian millennial teaching and it reveals whether we know what to expect based on doing the homework that Jesus Christ assigned: Post-tribulation Premillennialism doctrine holds that there is a resurrection-rapture of living believers in Jesus Christ at the end of the age (or the "End time"). Post-tribulationists believe that Christians will remain on the Earth through the three and a half year great tribulation period. This period starts at the Abomination of Desolation and ends at the Battle of Armageddon. They will be gathered by the angels to meet Christ in the air (raptured) at Christ's second coming immediately after the great tribulation just before the battle of Armageddon and then return with Him as Christ descends to the Earth, to usher in the Millennium (World to Come) on earth. This is usually understood as being in line with historic Premillennialism. Matthew 24:29-31 and 1 Thessalonians

4:15-17 parallel passages from Mark 13:24-27 and Luke 21:20-28. While the passages in Luke 21 parallels Matthew and Mark, it offers a couple of interesting clarifications. This passage in Luke offers interesting references to some of the major events which are greatly elaborated on in the Book of Revelation. Reading all three Books of the Bible in parallel, it would appear that Luke elaborates on the "abomination of desolation" describing Jerusalem being surrounded by the armies of the world and of Jerusalem's imminent destruction (Luke 21:20).

Another account which lends support to the idea of a post-tribulation rapture is in 2 Peter 3:10-13, where the idea of the "Day of the Lord" coming as a "thief in the night" comes from. This idea of imminence, according to the post-tribulation view, only applies to the wicked and the spiritually unprepared people that are still alive before the Return of Christ. Therefore, only God's elect (Christians) will fully have a clear understanding of the timing of the second coming, and therefore Christ's coming will not catch the believers by surprise, but only those who are spiritually ignorant regarding the truth. Pre-tribulational (dispensational) Premillennialism theology of dispensationalism consists of a distinctive eschatological end time's perspective, as all dispensationalists hold to Premillennialism and most hold to a pretribulation rapture.

Dispensationalists believe that the nation of Israel is distinct from the Christian Church, and that God has yet to fulfill his promises to national Israel. These promises include the land promises, which in the future world to come result in a millennial kingdom and Third Temple where Christ, upon his return, will rule the world from Jerusalem for a thousand years. In other areas of theology, dispensationalists hold to a wide range of beliefs within the evangelical and fundamentalist spectrum.

Postmillennialism is an interpretation of chapter 20 of the Book of Revelation which sees Christ's second coming as occurring *after* (Latin *post-*) the "Millennium", a Golden Age in which Christian ethics prosper. Although some postmillennialists hold to a literal millennium of 1,000 years, other postmillennialists see the thousand years more as a figurative term for a long period of time. Postmillennialism also teaches that the forces of Satan will gradually be defeated by the expansion of the Kingdom of God throughout history up until the second coming of Christ. This belief that good will gradually triumph over evil has led proponents of postmillennialism to label themselves "optimillennialists".

It has been criticized by 20th century political conservatives as an attempt to Immanentize the eschaton. Trying to bring about the eschaton (the final, heaven-like stage of history) in the immanent world. It has been used by conservative critics as a pejorative reference to certain utopian projects, such as socialism, communism, and transhumanism. In all these contexts it means "trying to make that which belongs to the afterlife happen here and now (on Earth)" or "trying to create heaven here on Earth."

Amillennialism teaches that there will not be a future "millennium" in which Christ will reign on earth prior to the Second Coming but rather that Jesus is presently reigning from heaven, seated at the right hand of God the Father, that Jesus also is and will remain with the church until the end of the world, as he promised at the Ascension, that at Pentecost, the millennium began, as is shown by Peter using the prophecies of Joel, about the coming of the kingdom, to explain what was happening, and that, therefore the Church and its spread of the good news is Christ's Kingdom and forever will be.

Amillennialists cite scripture references to the kingdom not being a physical realm: Matthew 12:28, where Jesus cites his driving out of demons as evidence that the kingdom of God had come upon them; Luke 17:20-21, where Jesus warns that the coming of the kingdom of God can't be observed, and that it is among them; and Romans 14:17, where Paul speaks of the kingdom of God being in terms of the Christians' actions. In particular, they regard the thousand year period as a figurative expression of Christ's reign being perfectly completed, as the "thousand hills" referred to in Psalm 50:10, the hills on which God owns the cattle, are all hills, and the "thousand generations" in 1 Chronicles 16:15, the generations for which God will be faithful, refer to all generations. So, which description of the future will be correct? The theories listed identify the possibilities and this means it is up to the actions of the body of believers to determine the exact nature of the second coming. Will the body of believers do the homework?

What is the purpose of the Lord's Prayer? When a terrorist explodes a bomb and kills an innocent eight year old boy many still ask, "What is the meaning of life"? The purpose and meaning of life is a call for the believers to take action. Life is full of choices and when we choose to not pray on Earth as it is in Heaven, then Adults will feel the punishment associated with sin. Prayer is how Jesus healed the sick, spoke to the sea, and defeated Satan. It was not Jesus Christ's will he did not act alone. Prayer is how the unexpected gets accomplished. Does God love or care about this world? If no, then pain is an imagination and life on Earth is meaningless. If yes, then life on Earth is meaningful. What are you supposed to do to make life more meaningful? The Lord calls us in his prayer to bring Heaven to Earth. The more you understand that God loves this world, the more you will begin to see how simple yet complex life is and encourage others to make a choice and bring Heaven to Earth.

The Lord's prayer is a constant reminder to lead us not into temptation but deliver us from evil. Many Christians believe that Jesus will come again before evil will be defeated or completely removed from Earth. Now my heat is troubled, and what shall I say? Father save me from this hour? No it was for this reason I came to this hour. Father glorify your name! Now is time for judgment on this world; now the prince of this world will be driven out.(John12:27-31) How will this occur? In a finite universe humans think of time in a linear sense. The past, present, and the future, thus it seems that when Jesus states that now the prince of this world will be driven out that the now means present. In an infinite universe, only the present exists! Do your homework and John 15:10 will become the now in your life! If you choose not to do your homework, then John 15:6 is your destiny.

Our sun, a beneficial giant that rules our solar system and provides the energy that allows life to exist on Earth. Its mass is what keeps the Earth from flying off into the Milky Way. However, the sun will be the entity that eventually destroys our planet. When the Sun dies it will engulf the earth and all of the inner planets, resulting in our doom. The size of the star or its mass determines its death. Big stars collapse into black holes or extreme vortexes that rip matter to shreds. These large stars can also explode in supernovas (http://www.hcs.harvard.edu/~hsr/pdfsspring2007/goyalcenterlayout.pdf).

Our sun simply does not have enough mass to form a black hole or explode into a supernova. Instead, our sun will slowly run out of hydrogen and gradually grow larger and hotter into a red giant.

(About 4.5 billion of our suns could fit into NML Cygni that largest star currently known. That means 4.5 quadrillion Earth's could fit into NML Cygni. (4,500,000,000,000,000) Current us debt equals 17,000,000,000,000)

Eventually our sun will burn out and turn into a cold dark white dwarf star. During the expansion of the sun into a red dwarf, closer planets will be engulfed by the Sun, and the Earth will simply be vaporized. The words of the Preacher, the son of David, king in Jerusalem. Vanity of vanities, saith the Preacher, vanity of vanities; all is vanity. What profit hath a man of all his labour which he taketh under the sun? (Ecclesiastes 1:1-3) *Just like Hanukah in which the oil eventually ran out, our sun will eventually run out of fuel.* This is true of the oil that we use for fuel, since oil is a nonrenewable fuel taking over one hundred years to produce.

So, what makes life meaningful? For God so loved the world, that he sent his son not to condemn the world but to save it. God loves this world. For God this world is very meaningful. This is why you should do the will of God, since doing the will of God makes life meaningful. God is eternal and this is the key requirement to make a task meaningful. Any task in order to be truly meaningful must be eternal.

Why should Harvard and Ecclesiastes be quoted here? It is important for adults to understand that all we do will not be remembered here on Earth. Scientists say that life came to Earth in the form of bacteria or developed from nonliving elements on earth, because the human race will perish on the Earth. The human race will not find another planet that can be reached and lived on by our offspring. The teacher understood this and we need to be reminded that from a biological perspective life is meaningless. We don't remember what happened in the past, and in future generations, no one will remember what we are doing now Ecclesiastes 1:11.

I also tried to find meaning by building huge homes for myself and by planting beautiful vineyards. I made gardens and parks, filling them with all kinds of fruit trees. After much thought, I decided to cheer myself with wine. And while still seeking wisdom, I clutched at foolishness. In this way, I tried to experience the only happiness most people find during their brief life in this world Ecclesiastes 2:3-5.

Without heaven and hell life is truly meaningless. If we leave this planet and there is nothing else, then everything is truly meaningless. Thus for me and my house we will believe in the place called heaven where Jesus is king and true love lives and hell a place where there is no love. Why don't the rich give more away of what they have earned, since life is meaningless? Come on are the rich stupid, since they lack the common sense to understand that the Sun is going to vaporize the Earth? If it is common knowledge that the Earth is going to be vaporized and that the human race will perish due to the restraints of gravity, then why don't the rich give more to the poor? Yes, to a degree all humans are selfish. The rich man asked Jesus, what must I do to inherit eternal life? Jesus, said to receive the gift of salvation sell everything you have and give it to the poor. Love is an action word and boasting of your work does not show love for others as described in Ephesians 2:9. The rich man was a selfish man, since he could not see the meaning of working together to accomplish the will of God. Money can allow us to feel as though we are better than others! I have a big house and nice car, because I do important things... (Matthew 6:24) God is good and no one part of God is better than another. When we think that we should hold onto a part of God that is better than another, then that is evil. Evil is truly blind and it is unfortunate that many listen to it, because they will find their place in seclusion. The more you have, the more people come to help you spend it. So what good is wealth—except perhaps to watch it slip through your fingers (Ecclesiastes 5:11)!

Does our government teach the poor that they should give to others? Why is it important to give regardless of net worth? Why is the poor widow in the following account giving all that she has to help others? And there came a certain poor widow, and she threw in two mites, which make a farthing. And he called unto him his disciples, and saith unto them, Verily I say unto you, That this poor widow hath cast more in, than all they which have cast into the treasury: For all they did cast in of their abundance; but she of her want did cast in all that she had, even all her living. (Mark 12:42-44) It seems a little odd that the poor widow would give to help others, however giving teaches the giver to value what they have and be content. Also, giving teaches the giver to say no. Those who are poor can remain poor due to bad decisions, since they lack the discipline to say no to others because they do not feel close to God. A person who says yes to every decision regarding spending money can remain poor. Natural disasters and related events make the case for the poor always being a part of society. However, the government and the church should stress that being poor is not a destiny and that learning to give will produce a wiser and smarter individual.

When you make a promise to God, don't delay in following through, for God takes no pleasure in fools. Keep all your promises you make to him. Talk is cheap, like daydreams and other useless activities. Fear God instead Ecclesiastes 5:4-7. We should Love our enemies and pray for those who persecute us, just as Jesus Christ taught us. Jesus is not telling us to love Satan or pray to Satan. Therefore Satan (the antichrist) will not come as one of us in human form, since that would require Satan to take a form other than his original.

And it is a good thing to receive wealth from God and the good health to enjoy it. To enjoy your work and accept your lot in life—this is indeed a gift from God. God keeps such people so busy enjoying life that they take no time to brood over the past (Ecclesiastes 5:11). There was a little city, and few men within it; and there came a great king against it, and besieged it, and built great bulwarks against it: Now there was found in it a poor wise man, and he by his wisdom delivered the city; yet no man remembered that same poor man. Then said I, Wisdom is better than strength: nevertheless the poor man's wisdom is despised, and his words are not heard. (Ecclesiastes 9:14-16). God created people to be virtuous, but they have each turned to follow their own downward path (Ecclesiastes 7:29).

Accept Jesus Christ before you become fearful of falling and worry about danger in the streets; before your hair turns white like an almond tree in bloom, and you drag along without energy like a dying grasshopper, and the caper berry no longer inspires sexual desire. Accept Jesus Christ before you near the grave, your everlasting home, when the mourners will weep at your funeral. For then the dust will return to the earth, and the spirit will return to God because of Jesus Christ. Otherwise, your life is truly meaningless a chasing after the wind.

Because we have turned to follow our own downward path, thus acting on evil, therefore it is not possible for us to be called children of God alone. We are children of the devil when by doing his will and choosing to sin we display his behavior. Reconciliation does not occur after death, since the devil will call you his own. God will not reconcile with the Devil, since the Devil does not love God. He told Jesus, if he would bow down and worship him he would give him all the kingdoms of this world. Jesus did the will of God, thus he is without sin. God is full of truth and the Devil is full of greed. And in that greed, the devil lost understanding the nature of his creation. Evil is foolish, because it lacks comprehension and is unwise. To everything there is a season, and a time to every purpose under the heaven: A time to be born, and a time to die; a time to plant, and a time to pluck up that which is planted. (Ecclesiastes 3:1-2)

Will you witness the redemption? Furthermore in a finite universe humans think of time in a linear sense. The past, present, and the future, thus it seems that when Jesus states that now the prince of this world will be driven out that the now means time in the present tense. In an infinite universe, only the time in the present tense exists! Time in an infinite universe is defined by the continuous movement of matter and energy through space. Time equals distance divided by velocity. Do your homework and John 15:10 will become the now in your life! If you choose not to do your homework, then John 15:6 is your destiny.

Chapter 10

God will Provide

because we know that suffering produces
perseverance; perseverance, character; and
character, hope.

(Romans 5:3-4)

P ay attention to your feelings and what is happening around your
location, which translates to stay alert stay alive. While in the Army
this point was constantly being made to us. Accidents happen
even to those we might think are not accident prone. All it takes is a
distraction or desires to get the task done fast and poor judgments are
made, then problems result. Even in times like this God will provide. It
is very important to pay attention to your surroundings at all times, since
God will provide a sign when he is trying to make a point. God loves you,
so it is very important that you desire to listen to him at all time. Paul made
this point numerous times when he was being persecuted as a follower of
Jesus Christ. When I think of Paul, he reminds me that God will provide.

Everything happens for a reason, thus the question becomes how will you
address the event that occurred? Failure is what causes most to quit and
never develop a new gift. When bad things happen that is when Christ
is handing the cross to you and the question becomes will you pick it up
and turn something bad into good? So many good things have resulted in
my life from the Holy Spirit guiding my steps. These events have prepared
me for the good times.

Those who have done evil things have chosen to listen to the evil one, thus our response should be to help them see the truth and get revenge. (Romans 12:19) An act of revenge is the mask behind most crimes, thus reforming the criminal concerns teaching him or her that true revenge concerns not repeating what was done to them on others. When we seek true revenge it concerns not becoming like the one who caused us grief. (Hebrews 10:30) When Satan attacks us, he desires to make us resemble him. In the end, he wants to destroy those who listen to him since he wants all of the attention. Most bad criminals desire to kill themselves once caught, because Satan sees them as competition and this is why he is seen as the destroyer. He is such a ruthless destroyer that he attacks and convinces those who listen to him to kill them self. (Matthew 10:28) By killing them self they are refusing any reconciliation that God has to offer. Death is a punishment from God, when someone takes their life they are saying that God does not have that authority to punish them. Therefore any reconciliation with God is not possible. However, John 3:16 is the only hope. Thus the only way to heaven is through Jesus Christ.

In order to understand Adam and Eve, we should look at their children. Cain farmed the land, thus he worked hard for the admiration of others and received none. This upset him, since Abel was a sheep herder and appeared to work less and was content. In Genesis 4:3, Cain gave part of his harvest to the Lord, and Abel also gave an offering to the Lord. The Lord was pleased with Abel and his offering, but not with Cain and his offering. This made Cain so angry that he could not hide his feelings. In this story, Cain and Abel are acting just like Adam and Eve. Eve in this story is Cain, since she as well was not content with her original talents and chose to act against the will of God to do something about it. There is an old saying; the apple does not fall far from the tree. Cain was enraged, since no one cared about all he did, since he only cared about himself and desired others to see his offering as the best. Life is such a competition and observed easily or at its best at family gatherings. Jesus spoke of this concerning the right hand not knowing what the left hand is doing. And those who do good things in this world for the attention of others receive their reward on Earth, since they are modeling the behavior of original sin.

When someone says that I am a nice person, I say thank you. However, deep down I know that I am not a nice person. I am a very vengeful person.

Jesus Christ defeated evil, so when I act like him I know that I am getting my revenge. If someone does something to you that you don't like, then make a conscious act not to repeat that act on others. Most bullies were bullied them self. Our sinful nature has been passed down since Adam and Eve, therefore we have been repeating acts based on Satan's plan. I encourage you to take the lead and change your ways and be a Christ follower. If you do not take a conscious effort not to repeat an event that hurt you, then you will repeat a similar action on another. This behavior only promotes what caused you grief and leaves you with the feeling of a lack of revenge. Vengeance is mine says the lord, God will provide the forgiveness needed to obtain peace.

What does God will provide mean? God will provide should be an inspiration to make us desire to work harder. God will provide means we are working for God. We are seeking to do his will and he will provide. It is surprising how many will completely ignore the obvious. Then someone comes along and invents a silly band. So, what can be done to help improve our chances for our God to provide? Our family chose to move three years ago, we found a house and put a contract on it to purchase, even though our house had not sold. After about a month we started to stress, because we could not afford to make two house payments. So we prayed about the situation, and decided that we needed a set dollar amount and that any amount above that would go to a Christian missionary. We didn't tell anyone what we were doing; we just doubled our work efforts to keep the house clean and straight. A problem with having young children around pets is they tend to turn over the pet food. This can attract mice, they tend to live in the attic of the home, they will scratch or move around at night; we notice that this happened at the same time of our plan to help Christian missions. We doubled our efforts and killed the mice. We were on a mission to get the house sold, because we wanted to support Christian missions. That was our focus and when we were cleaning and straightening as much as we could for a cause greater than the sale of our home; the sale of our home happened smoothly. Faster than expected we closed and purchased our next home on the same day and God provided a significant amount to Christian missions.

In Mark 8:17-21 his disciples began to argue with each other because they hadn't brought any bread. Jesus knew what they were saying, so he said, "Why are you arguing about having no bread? Don't you know or understand even yet? Are your hearts too hard to take it in? 'You have eyes—can't you see? You have ears—can't you hear? Don't you remember anything at all? When I fed the 5,000 with five loaves of bread, how many baskets of leftovers did you pick up afterward?" "Twelve," they said. "And when I fed the 4,000 with seven loaves, how many large baskets of leftovers did you pick up?" "Seven," they said. "Don't you understand yet?" he asked them. God is always capable of doing far more than we believe. What is the moral to this story? If we do a simple dimensional analysis of this math problem and use the first feast as the conversion factor, then the second feast should have yielded 9.6 extra baskets of leftovers. However, only seven were collected. Numbers matter and this story makes that clear, more seed can produce more crops.

God will provide is an inspiration for us to work diligently for him. Money is not enough of an incentive for us to do our best when times are tough, since most high risk investments do not pay off immediately, which can affect our need for immediate gratification on the task at hand. I have never written a book, however God will provide. The journey for this book started over pro-life values, thus a percentage of author royalties will go to support women who are choosing not to have an abortion. Not doing anything will lead to depression, so when something happens that many think shouldn't have happened what will be the response?

When an idea presents itself with large financial decisions necessary and no guarantee of producing a profit, then for us inspiration is needed. The inspiration pushes us to examine all the possibilities, so the idea has the greatest chance of being a success. Spending money and working without being paid for us requires greater inspiration. Before our house sold, I began working on an invention for an ethanol distillation system for automobiles using E85.

Why should an invention for ethanol distillation or an idea for making medical costs more efficient be in this book? When the cost of fuel goes up because a hurricane or other natural disaster or a child of mine is hurt in an accident both result in financial costs like in the game monopoly. When bills have to be paid and the money is not there to pay them, then a new plan needs to be presented to prevent the costs from increasing in the future. This is an example of observing an event that resulted in bad conditions and seeking to make the conditions better for others in the future. Often people refer to those who innovated for the betterment of human life as a genius, however God will provide as he knows what he is doing.

Coal which is used to generate electricity and oil which powers our transportation are both nonrenewable resources since they take over 100 years to renew. Our future needs will be met by renewable resources, so I began examining the ethanol distillation process with an objective to make it more efficient than the current model. I needed inspiration to go forward in the project, thus as a veteran and knowing that we have a large population of homeless veterans in America I was drawn to support a cause to help them. Those who work and volunteer to help the homeless are truly an inspiration to me, since the second commandment given by Jesus concerns loving your neighbor as yourself. Homeless people tend to wander the streets and cause problems for the police; this is the reason a percentage of all royalties that I receive from the following invention will go to support a hand up and not a hand out at Christian Homeless missions. If nonrenewable resources will eventually run out, then why are we not committed to using them only as an emergency? The goal of Satan is to produce the ladder climber or the genius ladder builder. The ladder climber desires to be seen as the best at wealth accumulation and have a title of queen bee. The hive will not survive without the queen bee. The production of renewable resources will not be as profitable for the leaders in charge compared to using nonrenewable products. Nonrenewable products lead to the concept of supply and demand which will lead to price changes at the gas station.

At church, my youngest son fell on a chair and cut his head. We went to the closest medical care facility and he was treated by gluing the small cut. The total bill for the care was $1400. We are responsible with our insurance for $700. The problem is that we had no idea what the bill was going to be until two months later. The cut was at the center of his head and not in a vital location. We have attempted to get the cost of this bill lowered with little success. The problem is that we are forced to pay this bill or it will cause our credit rating to be lowered. This incident led to the concept of www.MedicalBillEstimate.com.

Tax payers who pay into the Medicare program have the right to expect our tax dollars to be spent with the least amount of waste possible. The issue concerning health insurance is that of a monopoly. It is absolutely poor management for a company that is supposed to employ the smartest people to not be able to give an estimate of care before care is given with non-life threatening injuries. Health care providers do not give a quick estimate, because that could cause the customer to leave and that would drive down profits. Moreover, providing a quick estimate makes the company innovate to create better methods to deliver care at a more affordable price. Insurance companies have created this monster with the attitude of bill me later. The bill us later approach is no longer working to keep costs low concerning heath care and it needs to change.

Do a simple search of medical bills online and you will find many people have no idea what their medical bill will be when they leave the hospital. In the future, Obama care will promote the need for people to get an estimate before care is given. Why? Obama care is not free. How would this work? The website would allow a person to enter their name and insurance number; then all of the mathematical information associated with the patient's insurance plan would provide the hospital with the ability to generate a computer estimate of the cost of the treatment. Hospitals already know the general cost of most services. Any new services that were not listed on the first estimate would be communicated to the patient before care is given. If hospitals are intentionally trying to take monetary advantage of people, then this new business will expose that monopoly, since a monopoly does not promote a method for the customer to shop around for a service needed at a better price. The objective here is to prepare the individual, so that they are aware of the costs. This would allow patients to shop around when trying to determine the method for their treatment. An app would be set up so that a Google map would give the patient the closest care facility and the cost for the procedure. Estimates could be guaranteed within 10% of the final bill. The goal is to promote competition.

What is in it for the hospital? The hospital would be able to predict before the patient arrives what to expect. A photo app would be associated with the APP to make the process simple to complete before the patient arrives at the medical care center. This would greatly benefit the patient in slowing wait times at the hospital, since the medical info would already be in the computer along with access to the patient's medical file. Their medical file could be associated with their insurance card number. The significance of the idea concerns letting people store their medical records on the Medical Bill Estimate website for free. The website acts as a tool to help the patient get the best price for care. Moreover, the site would need password protection like that of a bank. The site would make money from the hospital and insurance companies. Why would insurance companies pay money to www.MedicalBillEstimate.com? Insurance companies desire for their patients to choose the most economical care for their injury. This is the reason for in network and out of network Doctors. Our website will be set up to promote the most cost effective method for the patient. When our business can prove that it saved the insurance company money, then a small fee would be charged. Fees would be collected from the insurance companies when care is given. The insurance company would be billed showing the 5 care facilities that the patient had to choose from and the evidence showing that www.MedicalBillEstimate.com saved them money. The company will store the patient's medical files on the website, so that the patient can get the best care and the hospital would provide the patient with a flash drive so that their medical data could be easily transferred to their medical profile on the MBE website. The hospital will pay our company a small fee for bringing the patient to their business. Most of the work concerns developing the computer program for this idea. Everyone likes to compete. Capitalism is all about competition.

An APP for the website would be sold to the patient, since it would be designed to make the process easier to accomplish. The sale of the APP would help cover the cost its development. This is where money from the patient can be made. Insurance companies will list on the website their customers and the policy type. Why would they do that? This will help their customer save money and increase their profits by decreasing waste. Our objective is to help them make more money, by preventing their customer from making a decision that would cost the insurance company more money. This information would be confidential and only accessible to the insurance company that places it on the website. Hospitals will be able to list on our website how much they will charge for a service, this will be confidential information made available only to the patient in the area of service. They will have a password and be able to modify costs.

Security for our website is a must, otherwise it will not work. This company needs to be global in its business operations, since patients will travel to get the best care. Patients are known to leave Canada and come to the US to get immediate care. The business model in Europe would center on the government and hospitals, since Hospitals send the bill to the government. The goal would be to keep costs low for the government. Hospitals should compete to keep costs low. If people know what the estimate of the bill that their government will likely have to pay, they will generally choose the most economical method. Why? They know that taxes go higher when waste occurs. This is our target for Medicare. We need to target the government as well, patients need to know the cost of the bill and try to keep those costs as low as possible in order to keep TAXES low. Persons that needed more immediate care would dial a 3 digit emergency number directly to www.MedicalBillEstimate.com/ where an operator would provide the patient with the most efficient options for care. A service fee would be charged to the phone of the patient for this care. Health care costs continue to grow faster than inflation, thus something has to be done to manage hospitals more efficiently. Hospitals and physicians account for majority of cost increases. http://www.unitedhealthgroup.com/hrm/UNH-Health-Care-Costs.pdf

Medicare does not have a maximum out of pocket expense, if a person with few resources saved has a medical bill of $100,000 they are responsible for paying $20,000.

US007910358B1

(12) **United States Patent**
Steineker

(10) Patent No.: **US 7,910,358 B1**
(45) **Date of Patent:** **Mar. 22, 2011**

(54) **ETHANOL DISTILLATION SYSTEM**

(76) Inventor: **David T Steineker**, Prospect, KY (US)

(*) Notice: Subject to any disclaimer, the term of this patent is extended or adjusted under 35 U.S.C. 154(b) by 867 days.

(21) Appl. No.: **11/850,254**

(22) Filed: **Sep. 5, 2007**

(51) Int. Cl.
C12M 1/00 (2006.01)
C12M 3/00 (2006.01)
(52) U.S. Cl. **435/289.1**
(58) Field of Classification Search 435/289.1
See application file for complete search history.

(56) **References Cited**

U.S. PATENT DOCUMENTS

4,407,955 A	10/1983	Muller et al.	
4,460,687 A	7/1984	Ehnstrom	
4,571,534 A	2/1986	Cover	
4,952,503 A	8/1990	Granstedt	
7,326,765 B1 *	2/2008	Tzap et al.	528/423

2002/0103548 A1 *	8/2002	Treiber et al.	700/30
2003/0175948 A1 *	9/2003	Hong et al.	435/289.1
2004/0044087 A1	3/2004	Maye	
2004/0087808 A1 *	5/2004	Prevost et al.	554/9
2004/0226451 A1 *	11/2004	Diaz	99/276

* cited by examiner

Primary Examiner — Walter D Griffin
Assistant Examiner — Shanta G Doe
(74) *Attorney, Agent, or Firm* — Crossley Patent Law; Mark A. Crossley

(57) **ABSTRACT**

An ethanol distillation system that aims to increase the yield from an ethanol distillation process from 17 percent to a number approaching 100 percent through the use of a series of P-traps, condensers, heaters and coolers. A series of 4 P-traps are placed in-line in relation to one another, with exit lines exiting each P-trap. Each P-trap has its own pair of heating elements and a single distillation apparatus, with the distillation apparatus condensing evaporated alcohol into liquid form and placing it into the exit line so it can be collected. Any liquids left over after it has passed through the series of 4 P-traps and a cold condenser will enter into a return pipe to be reused by the yeast in this process.

4 Claims, 2 Drawing Sheets

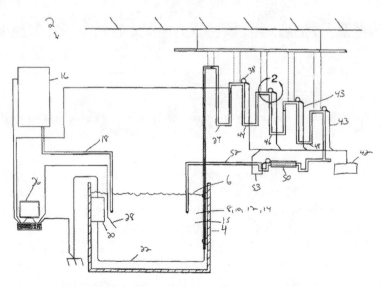

Click here to view Patent No. US 7,910,358 B1

(This ethanol distillation system is designed to breed yeast and support peak ethanol production limiting the death and growth phase which consumes ethanol and wastes resources.)

The above system is designed to be more efficient, because it works to keep the yeast alive instead of just focusing on ethanol production. Taking better care of the yeast and understanding how they work will make them more efficient, thus yield more ethanol with less energy expenditure in the distillation process. The most important part of playing any game is to field the best players. There are many different varieties or species of yeast; part of the research that has yet to be done for this invention concerns getting the best yeast for the process. The goal is to get yeast that can live and produce ethanol fast at or above 20% ethanol fermentation concentration. Higher ethanol concentration upon distillation requires less heat or energy. This system moves the liquid while it is being heated and subjects it to a water fall which naturally encourages liquid to gas formation. The biggest waste in the production of ethanol is in the distillation process and that is what this invention aimed to address.

(Distillation is a method of separating mixtures based on differences in volatility of components in a boiling liquid mixture. Students demonstrate an understanding of distillation.)

The above picture illustrates the reasons distilleries triple distill the fermentation wash. The goal of the invention is to breed yeast, so that they can live and produce alcohol at higher concentrations. Distillation is much more energy efficient when ethyl alcohol concentrations are above 15% in the fermentation wash. Currently, the industry distills the fermentation wash with the first step being to separate the mixture into water and ethyl alcohol. The problem with this system is that too much energy is being wasted boiling water.

The plan is to get the ethyl alcohol out of the fermentation wash at a vapor temperature between 85 and 93 degrees Celsius. To aid this process would involve converting the corn to corn syrup which would insure that all of the sugar will be used in the process. The key to making a profit consistently involves understanding the importance of preventing waste. Starches gellinate when heated so they can't be placed in the ethanol system that has been designed; this Ethanol Distillation System is similar in design concept to aquariums that keep fish alive. Take out the waste, keep the fish alive. For yeast, the waste is ethanol. However, the extraction has to be specific since yeast can eat ethanol when exposed to oxygen. Our objective is to produce low cost fuel, by getting the best yeast to produce ethanol and using this system to extract it in the most efficient way. The idea makes sense, yet it has not been proven to be profitable.

The point is that the distillation system could be a complete failure or it could be a dynamic success. How efficient the system is depends on a number of variables that have yet to be examined. Taking an idea to the patent pending level is not cheap; a large amount of money was spent with no guarantee of a profit. Writing and publishing a book meet similar criteria, since money is spent with no idea if anyone will purchase the book to recover the cost of printing it. Risks require inspiration, just like when Peter called to him, "Lord, if it's really you, tell me to come to you, walking on the water." "Yes, come," Jesus said. So Peter went over the side of the boat and walked on the water toward Jesus. But when he saw the strong wind and the waves, he was terrified and began to sink. "Save me, Lord!" he shouted. Jesus immediately reached out and grabbed him. "You have so little faith," Jesus said. "Why did you doubt me?" When they climbed back into the boat, the wind stopped. Then the disciples worshiped him. "You really are the Son of God!" they exclaimed. There is a huge point to this scripture reference where it concerns taking a risk. If the risk taker develops a sense of self pride about the task, then he or she will begin to fail or sink into the water like Peter because the distractions become greater than the inspiration.

Are you ready to be tested? Jesus prepares us to be tested, because he desires us to be strong leaders. Peter is a perfect example, since Peter was a disciple of Jesus and denied knowing Him during the crucifixion. Following this event Peter was put to the test and the Church was built on his refusal to deny the truth. Peter's request to be crucified upside down was his testimony to not my will Father but your will be done. Peter witnessed Jesus being crucified and rising from the dead the third day. Following this event, the world did not embrace what Peter had witnessed. The question is how will you respond when you are tested? Peter, like John the Baptist is a testimony to the word being more valuable than money. Often in life we put our faith in money as a means of power and protection. If you don't have money, then most would say that you can't be trusted; if people don't say it publicly, then they will say it in their actions. However, we are all one day away from absolute poverty. Just follow the news concerning recent earth quakes, floods or bank failures.

Blessed are the poor in spirit, because they are submissive in spirit. What makes us rich is our desire to give to others. Jesus pointed this out concerning the widow who gave even though she had very little money. Giving teaches the giver to say no to the things they view as luxuries. Stuff does not make one content. When God provides, people get inspired and are amazed at what can be accomplished. Are you prepared to accept the challenge, since everything happens for a reason? The challenge will reveal hypocrisy or character and which one leads to hope that produces confidence? If you r confidence comes from pleasing people, then hypocrisy will be the product. Mom and Dad have the potential to produce a child, if a child is produced does their confidence come primarily from pleasing the child? Kids will judge their parents more than anyone else they judge in life. We act like Satan when we desire to be the parent or commander and chief of everyone. (John 12:43) God knows what he is doing and does not need to be told what to do.

Chapter 11

The Chain of Command

If your actions inspire others to dream, learn more,
do more and become more, you are a leader."

John Quincy Adams

What did the voice of God sound like to Adam and Eve in the Garden of Eden? (Colossians 1:15-17) What does God look like and what are his expectations? The chain of command in heaven is circular and Jesus is the strongest link in the chain, since Jesus reveals this to us by saying I no longer call you servants, because a servant does not know his masters business. Instead, I have called you friends, for everything I have learned from my Father I have made known to you. The devil rules with a linear chain of command and has no friend's only servants.

As a descendant of original sin we are initially servants bound to sin. One of the experts in the law answered him, "Teacher when you say these things, you insult us also." (Luke 11:45) Why did Jesus insult those who were just trying to do their best? God made Jesus and he has consistently chosen to do the will of the God (Luke 22:42). Jesus spoke to the stormy waters and they became still. To the disciples' amazement, Jesus only had to speak a few words, and the storm became silent. The wind stopped and the water was still. He spoke and the sea obeyed. In order for the sea to obey it must be capable of following an order. If Jesus told you to sit in a chair, then you would need to hear the order in a language you could understand.

Understanding the importance of the chain of command rests on the power of choice to obey or follow an order. (Luke 22:42) The main point here is that God knows what he is doing. Humans we tend to think only in the terms of a human chain of command, the problem here is that in a human chain of command humans are only in charge of other humans. Humans don't have a chain of command to communicate with the sea or plant life. God has control of everything in the Universe and this is why Luke 22:42 is so important to understanding why the hierarchy we build up for ourselves and our ego is pointless. The sea, rocks, plants listened to Jesus because God can be understood and even the rocks will cry out to prove this point. (Luke 19:40) When God is described as uncomprehend able Jesus is being left out of the picture resulting in the meaning of life being misunderstood.

An eternal utopia of sameness would be a description of Jesus being left out of the picture, because a universe filled with only dark matter and nothing would be boring and expected. The chain of command is responsible for producing the unexpected, because each part in any molecule works as a team to promote diversity. Something being able to promote diversity would not be expected. Nothing is limited in diversity, since nothing lacks the ability to produce anything different. Something analogous to one type of leg-go would be expected to be limited in diversity. Moreover, something is unexpected to work together to produce visible matter like the Sun.

Woe to you, teachers of the law and Pharisees, you hypocrites! You shut the kingdom of heaven in men's faces. You yourselves do not enter, nor will you let those enter who are trying to. (Matthew 23:13) Saul was a practicing Pharisee and persecuted many Christians, then he experienced punishment for his sin (Acts 9:9). Jews at this time believed that if you got sick or a disease that you were not following God's will or the law. Saul was not naive. His thinking was associated with the fact that people can be wild and without law there is chaos. Saul could give an excellent account of all the gossip outside of the synagogue with humans doing whatever they pleased and he felt that Jesus was promoting this type of behavior. The Pharisee judged themselves as just doing the best they could. So, why did Jesus call them hypocrites? The Pharisee were using the law no different than a government uses the law to protect the wealth of the establishment. The United States government tries to prevent this with term limits for the president, however most business decisions are made by the Senate and House of representatives both of whom should have term limits since special interest groups can cause the needs of the people to become self-centered. The Pharisee were promoting a self-centered lifestyle that concerned seeking the best perks and other convinces no different than US senators have excellent health care and other retirement benefits. The poor person most often does not become a Senator, so catering to the wealthy promotes a society in which I should only look out for myself and my financial interests. The meaning of life concerns the creation of the eternal spirit, which is accomplished by following Jesus command as stated in John 15:12-15 and this is the reason Jesus called the Pharisee hypocrites. They were not promoting self-sacrifice as stated in Matthew 16:24, and Acts 17:11 which is required by both the financially poor and rich. The poor can be just as selfish as the rich and result in few talents being taken seriously.

The chain of command is associated with promoting children of the light, since God creates the unexpected. It would be expected that the reader should not exist and that only something and nothing would populate the universe. Building atoms from the three simple building blocks is not easy, proven by the fact that very few synthetic elements exist and the ones that have been created decay quickly. God knows what he is doing and when we desire to control the chain of command by being at the top as the Chief Executive Officer, then our goal becomes do whatever it takes to become God. When we seek to control anything in the chain of command that God created, then we are seeking to be God.

When we put Jesus up on a pedestal and declare that all the decisions he made were his, then we are indicating that we desire the same treatment and want others to listen to us with the same authority. We want to be a part of the chain of command, however not at the bottom of that chain. We want desperately to be a part of the main chain that sets us apart and designates us as title worthy.

God knows what he is doing. This is the most incredible thing about God. God controls his movement, he controls what he desires to build and he made Jesus. When Jesus says God not my will but yours be done he declares that the narrow path concerns doing the will of God and few find it. However many choose to follow the wide path that reflects our own will as being separate and praiseworthy from the rest of all creation. When we do our own will we are seeking personal glorification separate from the rest of creation.

Mark 11:12 On the next day, when they had left Bethany, He became hungry.

> Mark 11:13 Seeing at a distance a fig tree in leaf, He went to see if perhaps He would find anything on it; and when He came to it, He found nothing but leaves, for it was not the season for figs.

> Mark 11:14 He said to it, "May no one ever eat fruit from you again!" And His disciples were listening.

Mark makes it clear that it was not the season for figs; however Jesus could have easily instructed the tree to bear fruit. The point here is that the tree knew what season it was and its DNA instructed it how to react. Plants are a living thing, thus they complete a cycle and are ordered. Jesus did not want this to be dismissed as just another miracle. He wanted to make it clear to us that the fig tree was capable of following an order. It never bear fruit again. That would have required the tree to have understood what Jesus said to it. God wants you to understand that he knows what he is doing and this is the reason even the rocks would cry out in support of Jesus. "I tell you," he replied, "if they keep quiet, the stones will cry out." Luke 19:40 Why would the rocks cry out? The rocks are a creation of God, just like the plant; both the rock and the plant are necessary for us to build a home and to live. Without plants humans would die, kind of funny how humans can act so independent.

An ignorance of the fact that the human body and spirit are a creation of God will lead to the desire to become God. This behavior is not new as stated in John 8:42-47. John 8:58 states I tell you the truth before Abraham was born, I am. Those who obey Jesus commands as stated in John 15:9 are God's children, since they are children of the resurrection. (Luke 20:36) Jesus stated that in the resurrection humans will be "as angels" and "equal to the angels" (Matthew 22:29-30, Luke 20:35-36.) In Genesis 18:2,7-8,16 and 19:3 we find angels eating, but humans can also eat the food of angels (Psalms 78:23-25). In Genesis 19:10,16, Acts 12:7, Isaiah 6:6-7, Daniel 8:18, and Matthew 28:2 we find angels touching human beings and other physical (earthly) items. And in the same way angels are not (usually) visible to us and do not (usually) interact tangibly with things on the earth but instead are able to be visible and tangible from time to time, Jesus was also able to appear suddenly in rooms with locked doors (John 20:19,26.) After the resurrection, the difference between humans and angels will disappear completely as resurrected humans shall be like the resurrected Christ Jesus (1 John 3:2) They are God's children, since they are children of the resurrection. (Luke 20:36)

The chain of command in heaven is circular and Jesus is the strongest link in the chain which is opposite of the Devil and his linear chain of command in Hell. The Devil makes it so that those on top can get what they want and money is used to buy the best lawyer to defend any judgment against them. It is much easier for the rich to get away with a crime, because the devil is beautiful in appearance and seeks others to behave as beauty acting badly. A linear chain of command led the Pharisee to think that Jesus threated to destroy the temple building and labeled him as a terrorist. Jesus beating and crucifixion were meant to be a statement by the Pharisee to anyone who threatened to destroy the temple that immediate death would result. Jesus stated that woe to you teachers of the law and Pharisees, you hypocrites! You travel over land and sea to win a single convert, and when he becomes one, you make him twice as much a son of hell as you are. The Pharisee were using a linear chain of command, just like the devil. Get that one convert and make him do everything to make you look holy.

The chain of command in heaven is circular and Jesus is the strongest link. In a circular chain of command everyone is working to make the weak link stronger, and even the gates of hades shall not prevail against it. Those seeking to get to the top of the ladder desire to lead their own way and tell others to stay the course. In a linear chain of command Jesus would have never been able to leave heaven and come to Earth, since the Angels in heaven would act like a teenager that desires to be the leader of the house. In a linear chain of command those beneath only obey because they have to obey and they long for the day when they will receive their inheritance or be on top. The best scripture evidence for a circular chain of command is when Jesus states, "receive the Holy Spirit; If you forgive anyone his sins, they are forgiven; if you do not forgive them, they are not forgiven."

Now some of the teachers of the law were sitting there, thinking to themselves, "Why does Jesus Christ talk like that? He is blaspheming! Who can forgive sins but God alone?" (Mark 2:6-7) If Heaven had a linear chain of command, then Jesus would not have given authority through the Holy Spirit to forgive sin and promote peace. For the forgiveness of sin promotes peace and an eye for an eye promotes war. Again Jesus said, "Peace be with you!" As the Father has sent me, I am sending you." (John 20:21)

Chapter 12

Child of God

Life's purpose in Christianity is to to seek divine salvation through the grace of God and intercession of Christ.

(John 11:26)

They are Gods children, since they are children of the resurrection. (Luke 20:36) This is the meaning of Life: God created us on this Earth for the primary purpose of producing the eternal spirit as a child of God. The free dictionary defines wisdom as the ability to discern or judge what is true, right, or lasting; insight. Wise decisions produce lasting results. (Luke7:35) "It is a characteristic of wisdom not to do desperate things". (Henry David Thoreau) After some study one might begin to feel as though they have learned enough, then one gets sick. Sickness is a sign of weakness and nature puts to death the weak animals rather quickly. The lion looks for the weak ready to pounce, kill, and devour an easy meal. Then death and Hades were thrown into the lake of fire. The lake of fire is the second death. If anyone's name was not found written in the book of life, they were thrown into the lake of fire. (Revelation 20:14) But the cowardly, the unbelieving, the vile, the murderers, the sexually immoral, those who practice magic arts, the idolaters and all liars their place will be in the fiery lake of burning sulfur. This is the second death. (Revelation 21:8) When the lion eats its meal, the flesh of the prey is broken down in the stomach all the way down to the primary building blocks of life and reassembled into new lion protein, fat, and DNA. Likewise, the human body must breakdown chicken protein so it can be reassembled and stored as human protein.

Death is an ending. The second death is where the spirit ends, since its name is not found in the book of life. The lake of fire is analogous to the stomach of the lion. The building blocks of the spirit are reassembled at a point between inner course and the third week after conception. Even though the organs associated with an orgasm are located near the belly, the majority of the euphoric sensation occurs in the mind. According to WebMD, the fastest sperm can get to a fallopian tube is about 30 minutes, meaning that the quickest conception could occur following sex is in the half-hour range. It can take up to seven days after intercourse for sperm and egg to join and become a fertilized egg. Usually, it's because the sperm gets into the fallopian tube before the egg is released. The fifth week of pregnancy, or the third week after conception, marks the beginning of the embryonic period. This is when the baby's brain—Mind, spinal cord, Heart and other organs begin to form. Matthew 22:37 states that we are to love the Lord your God with all your heart and with all your soul and with all your mind. After the third week is when the human body takes on form. I knew you before I formed you in the womb; I set you apart for me before you were born; I appointed you to be a prophet to the nations. (Jeremiah 1:5) This is the meaning of life: the formation of the spirit with the primary purpose of it accepting John 3:16. Angels are different from us, since they have not experienced the physical death of a loved one; and physical death is a warning to your spirit. In loving memory of Gretchen Hall Ralston, October 4, 1975-January 24, 2013.

What is the purpose of life? Is the flesh more important than the spirit? Not knowing what occurs after death makes us think that the flesh is more important and leaves us with no answer to what is the meaning of life. Solomon concluded that we should love God and follow his commands; however Solomon does not mention grace. This has led some to believe that Solomon may not even be in Heaven. (http://www.enduringword. com/commentaries/1111.htm)

When the body dies, then doubts arise about the strength of the spirit. If the spirit is not eternal, then life has no meaning for the individual. God created us on this Earth for the primary purpose of producing the eternal spirit. Some believe that their spirit was created in Heaven and came to Earth upon conception. This leads to the question what initiated the spirit conception in heaven and why? This has serious consequences for the meaning of life on Earth. If your spirit was not created upon conception on Earth, then that spirit coming from Heaven would be a form of Reincarnation. The spirit formed in Heaven would not have the inherited sin from Adam and Eve. That spirit would be without sin having come out of heaven. Therefore, why would that spirit have any desire to leave Heaven and come to Earth to have its sins forgiven? A spirit formed in Heaven leaves what Jesus Christ did on Earth meaningless! God would not have needed to create Jesus, if our spirit was formed in Heaven and came to Earth. This is the primary reason those who believe in reincarnation don't see the meaning in accepting Jesus Christ to save them from their sin. In a finite Universe life is meaningless, since truth and lies are the same resulting from something and nothing being interchangeable.

The spirit formed before live birth would have the inherited sin which occurred on Earth. In an infinite Universe something and nothing are eternal, thus something is capable of making life meaningful. The tricky part of understanding the meaning of life concerns the formation of the spirit before live birth. Substances that have a birth are finite and thus the spirit should have a death. In an infinite Universe, time is a continuum. This means that something has always existed and an infinite Universe does not follow the linear timeline we have based our life upon. A linear time line has a past, followed by a present, then a future. An infinite universe only has a present state, since it is continuously in motion and lacked a beginning and never will end. This may seem odd, however mathematically it makes complete sense based on the logic that one and zero are opposites. Something and nothing must be opposites for zero to not equal one. Therefore, an infinite universe is continuously in motion. Moreover, the tricky part of understanding the meaning of life concerns the formation of the spirit before live birth.

The Bible states that Heaven and Earth will pass away. (Matthew 24:35) The point is that for life to have meaning the spirit must be eternal. Atheists do not believe that there is a heaven or hell after death, thus they believe that once you die that nothing occurs afterward. Those who believe in reincarnation do not see a need for accepting Jesus, since the human spirit wants us to think we are better than others and that eventually we will show that and climb the mountain and reach the top on our own. So, what does this have to do with Matthew 24:35? As a Christian, we should believe that life exists after Heaven. God is in control and in an infinite universe; God has the power to change anything and Christians would be no different than Atheists if we choose to believe that life does not exist after Heaven as stated in Matthew 24:35. Otherwise, everything done including Jesus death on the cross would be meaningless. Jesus makes it clear in Matthew 10:35 and Luke 12:49-59 that it will be difficult on your spirit to not see some of your loved ones in heaven. Love is measured in our response to action, thus expect heaven to be full of love. Those who hold on to John 3:16 will experience eternal life where ever he leads us, he knows the way. (John 8:51) The question will remain do you desire eternal life? (John 8:51) The spirit is a Holy ratio of something "God" and it was created to be Eternal. In a continuum, something is in perfect balance with nothing. The point is that something "God" created the spirit to be eternal, therefore John 3:16 is the scripture verse that defines the meaning of life.

If there is a desire for life to be meaningful, it has to be eternal otherwise there would be no memory or reference that you were ever here on Earth. There would be no purpose to life, since there would be no reason to be good. Truth and lies would be the same and anarchy would eventually prevail. Spirits that do not accept John 3:16 will not be eternal based on Proverbs 4:23, Matthew 10:35, Luke 12:53, 1 Peter 5:8, John 10:10, and Revelation 12-15; these scripture versus state the importance of following Jesus, so that your spirit will not end otherwise the Devil will destroy your spirit. A spirit that was created new upon conception was created from the building blocks of those spirits that refused to accept John 3:16. Where is the proof? Life on this planet is the proof. In a continuum, time is eternal. This means there has been enough time to create spirits out of every bit of something in the Universe. Love is a choice and it is your choice to be eternal. I desire to be eternal, because of Jesus Christ. His word is true, I admire his love, and I am thankful for him providing the way. http://www. goodnewsaboutgod.com/studies/seconddeath2.htm

Luke 10:25-28 is the scripture reference for this chapter, because wise decisions produce lasting results. What is the meaning of life? Solomon struggled with this question and many have debated it with dubious answers. Is life about the struggle to succeed, so that we can receive praise from men? (John 12:43) Is the purpose of life to gain earthly wealth, so that we have the freedom to do as we please? Capitalism is an economic system that is based on private ownership of capital goods and the means of production of goods and services for profit. Is the purpose of life to be like Solomon and obtain the most profit? Most view Solomon as the wisest man that ever lived based on the exuberant wealth that he controlled. Is the purpose of life to obtain great wealth through a monopoly or pyramid scheme, then act as a philanthropist and give to those in need to show your generosity? (John12:43)

John the Baptist was the greatest man who ever lived, because he prepared the way and when the way is not prepared grace can't occur. Was John the Baptist wiser than Solomon? What did Solomon do that made him wiser than John the Baptist? John the Baptist did not live a life full of sin; he was born with a love of the Lord in his heart. He was not perfect in displaying love for his enemies; however Solomon lived a life full of sin. Therefore Solomon was the wisest man to ever live, because he publicly announced his failure to make wise decisions based on the law and sought forgiveness from God for the enormous amount of sin he committed in his lifetime by encouraging others to not follow his mistakes. Solomon's last words in Ecclesiastes are to Love God and obey his commandments, thus the book of Ecclesiastes is a book of repentance. The greater the amount of sin the more difficult it becomes to openly seek repentance, most like Judas will just end their life to prevent being publicly disgraced. Solomon's boldness to publicly acknowledge his sin is a display of wisdom and inspiration to all that fear their sin is too great to repent. Solomon encourages all who are in prison or have committed a crime to display the same courage. Solomon is the leader of wisdom or the wisest man who ever lived because he was man enough to admit the greatness of his sin, and through humility encouraged others not to follow his way.

It is important to review a little about Solomon, so that the message of Solomon's wisdom is explained correctly! In 961 B.C., Solomon, the son of David and Bathsheba, became the third king of Israel and under his leadership the wealth and prestige of his country steadily increased. He ruled a kingdom whose borders stretched from the River Euphrates to Philistia and the Egyptian border. Historians refer to this time as the high point of the Golden Age of Israel. The Bible characterizes Solomon as being richer and wiser than any other king.

King David had an affair with Bathsheba the wife of Uriah the Hittite, then David had Bathsheba's husband killed. (2 Samuel 11:5, 2 Samuel 14-17) The baby conceived due to the affair died, and David mourned the loss. (2 Samuel 13-19) "Then David comforted his wife Bathsheba, and he went to her and lay with her. She gave birth to a son, and they named him Solomon" (2 Samuel 12:24) Was David punished for the murder of Uriah the Hittite? Yes, he mourned the loss of the child and the Lord was not gracious by allowing the child to live. (2 Samuel 12:22)

This is important to understand, since Cain received punishment for killing Abel. Should we try to justify Solomon's action of killing his brother Adonijah by blaming Adonijah for being wrong to be proclaimed as king? Solomon had an older brother, and he was first in line to follow David as ruler of Israel. Adonijah was the name of his older brother; Adonijah means "my Lord is Yahweh." He was the fourth son of David, his mother was Haggith (2 Sam. 3:4). After the death of his elder brothers, Amnon and Absalom, he became the heir-apparent to the throne. His younger brother Solomon, however, was preferred over him to gain the thrown. Adonijah, however, when his father was dying, caused himself to be proclaimed king. But Nathan the prophet, and Bathsheba, Solomon's mother, convinced David to give orders that Solomon should at once be proclaimed king and seated on the throne. Adonijah fled and took refuge at the altar, and received pardon for his conduct from Solomon on the condition that he showed himself "a worthy man" (1 Kings 1:5-53)

David died after reining for king over Israel for 40 years. Solomon's time of co-regency with his father ended, and now Adonijah had the opportunity to show himself to be a worthy man. Adonijah made the request to be given Abishag, David's nurse as a wife, but he was quickly seized and put to death. (1 Kings 213-25) Abishag would have given Adonijah the inheritance needed to justify his kingship. Those who live by the sword die by the sword. The point is that Killing Adonijah removes the threat to Solomon's legacy. Now we never know what would have happened, if Adonijah were banished like Moses from Egypt. The desire to be seen as better than others fuels unwise decisions. What Solomon did is often justified by how many view Solomon's wisdom in financial decisions. (http://www.spwickstrom.com/adonijah/) Solomon's great worldly wealth is mentioned first in his description, so that we know he had authority.

I will surely tear the kingdom away from you and give it to your servant: God promised the entire kingdom of Israel to the descendants of David forever, if they only remained obedient. David reminded Solomon of this promise shortly before his death (1 Kings 2:4). Yet they could not remain faithful even one generation. For the sake of David, God delayed this judgment until after Solomon's generation. But the disobedience that brought the judgment came in the first generation.

Solomon was the wisest man to have ever lived, because he lived a life of sin and spoke of how it made him feel. His final conclusion stated in Ecclesiastes 12:13 is fear God and keep his commandments. Why is this important and how does it make him the wisest man to have ever lived. The fear of God is associated with loving God, since those whom you truly love yields a fear of not hurting them. I love you so much that I fear hurting you, thus my choices to follow the commandments are based on the love of God. Satan does not want you to understand this and seeks followers of the law to show others how good they are and Jesus will judge you as a hypocrite. For God calls us to first love all that is good and offers forgiveness to those who obey as Jesus states to all those who believe in John 3:16. Did the rich young ruler believe and receive eternal life? (Mark 10:22-23)

Chapter 13

The Unforgivable sin

You had the seal of perfection, full of wisdom and perfect in beauty

Ezekiel 28:12

Satan can be properly described as Beauty acting badly. Satan is an oxymoron and the author struggles most with his extreme jealousy at the human race. Genesis states that all was good until God created Adam and Eve. Satan knew Jesus as a friend, since Jesus existed before the creation of Adam and Eve and Jesus did not die on the cross to forgive the sin of Satan. Is there a sin that can't be forgiven?

Jesus Christ will not offer grace to those who do not love God, since Jesus did not forgive the sin of the devil on the cross. The devil has not been forgiven and that hell is a present place in existence based on the parable of the rich man and Lazarus. It does not state that in ten thousand years the rich man eventually goes to Hell or that Lazarus has to wait a million years with everybody else in a long line so that everyone can go to heaven at the same time. It does not state that hell will eventually be built.

It states upon death angels take Lazarus to Abraham's side. There was a rich man who was dressed in purple and fine linen and lived in luxury every day. At his gate was laid a beggar named Lazarus, covered with sores and longing to eat from the rich man's table. Even the dogs came and licked his sores. The time came when the beggar died and the angels carried him to Abraham's side. The rich man also died and was buried. In Hell, where he was in torment, he looked up and saw Abraham far away, with Lazarus by his side. (Luke16:19-23) Why did Jesus say that Lazarus was taken to the side of Abraham? According to the human chain of command only the King or commander in chief should have supreme authority to judge a life and forgive sin. In Proverbs 4:23 we are instructed to guard our heart, since everything done flows from it. As a descendant of original sin, we lack the authority to judge ourselves better than others; only Jesus has the authority to instruct us about the commands of God because his intentions purely teach that your best is never good enough as illustrated with the seven woes spoken to the Jewish leaders. Jesus commands us to love, so what does that mean? We really do want to be like Jesus, the problem is that our judgment of the sins of others like homosexuality allows the homosexual to in turn cast a judgment on the liar and call him or her a hypocrite. Do as I say and not as I do! When you die your life will be defined by Romans 6:23 and for this reason John 3:16 defines the meaning of life in the creation of the child of God, the eternal spirit. To sin less is still not good enough to be given the authority to judge others. Why is you best never good enough? Your best creates selfish ambition to control the team instead of working to make the weak link stronger. We really desire to control the team, which concerns climbing the ladder to get to the top and instructing others what is best. If others won't listen, then we build our own ladder or establish a new game to get others to follow our instructions.

What happens if the means are not available to build a new ladder, or if the skills are not there to make it above thirteenth place in a given race? We fall apart and become depressed, since the goal for Satan is to get others to mimic his behavior, because Adam and Eve chose to listen to Satan in the garden we have inherited his sinful nature. Where is the evidence for this statement? The total existence theory states that the universe is either finite or infinite allowing the reader to make a decision based on the mathematical conclusions a finite universe and infinite universe present. God knows what he is doing and trying to tell him what to do is an insult to God; the author believes that God is something that has mass and takes up space. So what is the point? Satan is a creation of God and he has chosen to tell God what to do. Satan is derived from the term accuser. The name Lucifer actually means Light Bringing and Morning Star. When the War in Heaven is spoke about in Revelation, the Lucifer is called Dragon, Satan and the Devil. As stated in Luke 10:18 "I saw Satan fall like lightning from

Heaven". Therefore, how much are you going to follow Satan and bring Hell to Earth? Satan does not care that you are a creation of God, since a third of the angels in heaven agree with him that he is more beautiful than you will ever be. Satan has no concern for the truth. The truth being that Satan is a creation of God defined by number and ratio. Moreover, Satan has no concern for your creation of God defined by number and ratio. The t John the Baptist was described by Jesus as being the greatest man that ever lived. So why does the Bible not mention Jesus crying at word of his execution? John the Baptist did not have the authority to speak to King Herod like Jesus did to the Jewish leaders, since John's death reflects a descent from original sin. (Romans 6:23)

Will there be those that committed murder in Heaven? Will there be those that lied in Heaven? Will there be those that stole from others in Heaven? Will there be homosexuals in Heaven? Yes, Yes, Yes, Yes... God does not require us to be good, He requires us to love all that is good. Will all homosexuals be in heaven? No. Will all liars and murders be in heaven? No. All will sin till their death, did you love your neighbor? The test is did you love your neighbor! (John15:17)

Is there a sin that can't be forgiven? Truly I tell you, people can be forgiven all their sins, and every slander they utter, but whomever blasphemes against the Holy Spirit will never be forgiven, they are guilty of an eternal sin. (Mark 3:29) It does not read everybody except those whom are baptized. It says whomever and just like the Pharisee whom cared more for the temple building many Preachers and Elders have followed the same path. Most people do not care if life is meaningless or that everything they do will be forgotten as spoke by Solomon in Ecclesiastes. Life can be a lot of fun, until others become jealous of material possessions and plan a robbery. Eventually something will happen that causes us to cast a judgment and make a change, so that we can prevent others from destroying our kingdom of fun. Why do parents have such a strong desire to separate the poor kid from the rich, the good soccer player from the poor soccer player, and the gifted student from the challenged student? If every person on the team has the same talent, then is it really a team or just a bunch of "Me". We could call it the "you're just like me team". The "you're just like me team" has the desire to win and will say those who say winning is not important have never won anything.

Unfortunately, the "you're just like me team" is really acting like the devil. Satan's language is look how good I am, look how pretty I am, and I should tell you what to do since you are not capable of making choices do to the fact that I am better than you. (Ezekiel 28:12) Blasphemy is an act of cursing or reviling God. If someone or something is reviled, people hate them intensely or show their hatred of them. God created the Universe by his movement through empty space, thus blasphemy of God can be measured in a tangible way as recorded in John 15:17.

Who cares about Mark 3:29, since telling the followers that all their sins will be forgiven keeps them happy and blind to real change? Money and a chain of command most often are used to display one person as being more important than another person. This chain of command is the most common used and it's the reason the devil is currently the ruler of this world. The devils chain of command is linear with the Devil sitting on top. The unforgivable sin is associated with Satan, so what does Satan look like and why does this matter?

Satan or the Devil was created as an anointed cherub. So Satan was created a cherub and he originally was "the anointed cherub that covered" the very throne of God. He was perfect and "blameless". Reading God's description in Ezekiel, you see all the precious stones that have ever been created are a covering of his: gold, emeralds, jasper, and so on. He was "full of wisdom and beauty" but his pride lifted up his self-worth and he became "unrighteousness" before God. Satan was of the highest rank of all angels created; greater in power and rank than Michael and Gabriel. The unforgivable sin, does this really matter, is it a sin that only a few people are committing; so should it just be ignored as insignificant?

Is the unforgiveable sin too complicated to understand? The Bible is so very important, because it reveals to us the sins that are forgivable and the sin that is not forgivable. Those who do not want to understand the unforgivable sin only want to judge others for the sin they commit like homosexuality. The unforgivable sin should not be ignored, since it is the sin that even the Christian will be judged upon; whomever blasphemies against the holy spirit means anyone who is found committing the unforgivable sin will not be forgiven.

Most Christians will think that they are free from judgment, which can lead those who are not Christian to judge them as arrogant. When one knows that they will be judged everything changes in the attitude of the sinner. Remember Satan will judge you or Jesus will forgive you and the choice is yours. Once in Heaven, forgiveness removes any remembrance of the sin committed. A judgment in court holds onto the sin or keeps a record of it especially one like murder.

Is Satan ugly? How often do we listen to ugly people? Are ugly people really that captivating, usually they are cast outs and ignored as not pretty to look at and maybe even to listen to because they had an ugly voice. American Idol spends a lot of time looking for that pretty voice. It is important to know what your enemy looks like so that you can better defend yourself from attack. Revelation describes Satan as a Red Dragon that stretches across a third of the Universe removing a third of the stars from heaven which is an analogy relating to Satan taking a third of the angels with him when he was cast out of Heaven. (Revelation 12:3-4) Then another sign appeared in heaven: an enormous red dragon with seven heads and ten horns and seven crowns on its heads. Its tail swept a third of the stars out of the sky and flung them to the earth. The dragon stood in front of the woman who was about to give birth, so that it might devour her child the moment he was born.

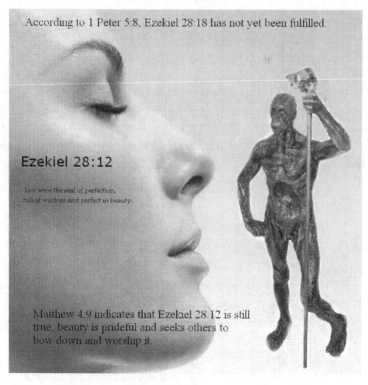

According to 1 Peter 5:8, Ezekiel 28:18 has not yet been fulfilled.

Ezekiel 28:12

You were the seal of perfection, full of wisdom and perfect in beauty.

Matthew 4:9 indicates that Ezekiel 28:12 is still true, beauty is prideful and seeks others to bow down and worship it.

(Beauty is prideful and seeks others to bow down and worship it as stated in Matthew 4:9.)

How can we know for sure that this description of Satan in Revelation is allegory? First there is no scripture verse that specifically states his appearance changed when he was cast out of heaven. If his appearance changed, then all of the angels following him would have returned to heaven. Looks can be very captivating and pornographic industry is well aware of this fact. Thus Satan's appearance did not change when he was cast out of Heaven, because Ezekiel would not have been able to describe him as beautiful had his appearance changed. Why? Satan would have spoken up and objected. When will Satan's appearance or look change?

The Bible says that Satan will continue in his rebellion against God until the very end. Near the end, a "beast" (world ruler) will arise from the "sea" (the gentile nations), having been given power by Satan to perform signs and wonders for the world. In addition, a false prophet, a religious leader empowered by Satan will deceive people into worshipping him. The beast and the false prophet will convince the leaders of the earth to follow them into war against God and His people. However, the armies of the leaders of the world will be destroyed at the battle of Armageddon and the beast and false prophet will be thrown into the Lake of Fire. At this point, Satan will be locked up for 1,000 years, while Jesus Christ rules the earth with His saints. At the end of that period, Satan is released for a short period of time, deceives the leaders of the world again, and convinces them to attack Jesus and His rule on the earth, his battle is short as fire from heaven consumes the rebels. Satan is then thrown into the Lake of Fire (hell) to "be tormented day and night for ever and ever." Following Satan's demise, the saints of Jesus Christ will judge the angels who joined him in rebellion.

Ezekiel 28:18 states that God has turned Satan to ashes in the eyes of all who see him. (Matthew 4:11) Ashes would be dust and the Ezekiel 28:18 reference to Satan's demise. Revelation and Ezekiel provide two references to Satan's demise similar to the four references to Jesus Christ's second coming: Post-tribulational Premillennialism, Pre-tribulational (dispensational) Premillennialism, Postmillennialism and Amillenialism. Since Jesus battled Satan and was tempted by him during his fast for forty days, thus evidence indicates that he is still in his cherub angelic appearance. Moreover, he is still capable of deception, since he offered Jesus authority to rule over all nations if Jesus bowed down and worshipped his angelic splendor. (Matthew 4:8-9)

In their heavenly state according to the Bible, a cherub is a large creature— up to 18 feet in height (1 Kings 6:23-28) with 8 foot long wings. (Exodus 25:20) In the prophet Ezekiel's vision, the cherubim (plural of "cherub") had four wings. (Ezekiel 10:8) Under their wings were human-like hands that could be used to carry things. All the surfaces of the cherubim, including the wings, were covered with eyes. (Ezekiel 10:21) Each cherub had four faces, one "of a cherub, the second the face of a man, the third the face of a lion, and the fourth the face of an eagle."

Was Jesus Christ naive? Nice people get taken advantage of at the workplace daily. If I know that all I have to do is accept Jesus and all my sins will be forgiven, then why not live as a wild ass all the way to the last second and accept Jesus. When the question is asked was Jesus Christ naïve it is associated with him being too nice to human beings. Do human beings take advantage of nice people? Yes. So, is Jesus Christ too nice? When humans take advantage of nice people they do not listen to them they try to figure out how to use them for their own personal gain. If Jesus were naïve, then people could live as wild asses all life and at the last second accept Jesus and be saved.

According to Satan there are two types of people in the world, the ladder climber, and the ladder builder. The ladder climber resembles Satan, because Satan desires to be seen as better or the best of God's creation and then to be worshipped. The ladder climber resembles this behavior with his or her attempt at being associated with doing anything better than anybody else. Most people desire to be on the winning team. There is nothing wrong with striving to do your best, it is not naive to think that one can do his or her best without striving to be like Satan. The ladder builder is often referred to as a genius. The Webster dictionary defines a genius as extraordinary intellectual power especially as manifested in creative activity. Thus the genius is the one who builds a new game or a new product. Thomas Edison would be described as a ladder builder or a genius. Is a prophet a genius? A prophet gives the credit to God as being the source of the truth, thus the prophet states that God knows what he is doing. A genius states that his or her hard work is the reason for the new product and that they deserve the credit for the accomplishment. Was Jesus Christ a ladder builder or a ladder climber? The Bible states in Luke 9:46 that his followers wanted to climb the ladder and be seen as the greatest.

Throughout the bible Jesus states that he was sent by God and he denies the throne that he could have taken here on Earth. This really confused the apostles following him and is the greatest evidence for his resurrection. Why? Jesus was taken to a cross to be crucified and his message would have been forgotten had he not risen from the dead. Miracles provide evidence that what Jesus says should be listened to and promoted. Matthew 17:16-21 provides the evidence that Jesus Christ is not a ladder builder, since he states that all he did happen because of prayer and fasting. Jesus Christ is not a ladder builder nor a ladder climber he is the Son of God, because he revealed the nature of God to us.

The Son of God states that God knows what he is doing and that we are required to love all that is good. Jesus constantly gives God credit for all that he accomplishes and this is the reason his prayers are always answered. (Matthew 17:16-21)

The purpose is associated with the title of this book and scripture verses have been given and parables noted that provide evidence that Jesus Christ the Son of God is not naïve and all will be judged and held accountable to the unforgivable sin. Heaven is not a fantasy land and it does require work to get there, since love is an action word. Love is something that you do, if you have no love for God then you have not used your God given talents out of fear of rejection or failure.

Those whom love God do not boast about what they have done, since that would contradict the definition of love. Matthew 8:20 and Luke 5:14 states then Jesus said to him, "See that you don't tell anyone. But go, show yourself to the priest and offer the gift Moses commanded, as a testimony to them." Matthew 16:20 states he ordered his disciples not to tell anyone that he was the Messiah. Ephesians 2:9 warns those whom boast, since that work would contradict the definition of love and resemble Satan. Love requires work, since it is an action word. Raising children requires a lot of work and my kids see it as love and sometimes tough love. Therefore, Jesus Christ requires work from us and as a parent I can tell you that he will not let you take advantage of him. Jesus is not naïve and blaming others for your ignorance will not set one free from being held accountable to the unforgivable sin.

God does not require us to be good as stated in Mark 10:17-27. In this passage the rich ruler states the he had followed all the commandments. Also, what is important about this scripture is the fact that Jesus states that only God is good. Jesus commands us to love, so what does that mean?

The purpose of the chain of command is to model it on Earth as it is in Heaven? So, what does the chain of command look like in Heaven? Is it linear, like the Devil in Hell is the commander in chief? No Jesus said," The world must learn that I love my Father and that I do exactly what my Father has commanded me." (John 14:31) Jesus said, "For whoever does the will of my Father in heaven is my brother sister and mother." (John 12:50) The chain of command in heaven is circular and Jesus is the strongest link in the chain. The sin inherited from the fall resulted in being defined as a servant of the devil, and Jesus death on the cross provides the way to be a friend of God. The greatest commandment states that we are required to love all that is good and the unforgivable sin means that we will be held accountable to the greatest commandment.

Proverbs 4:23

References

1. Judith Campisi Ph.D. "Telomeres." http://mcb.berkeley.edu/courses/mcb135k/telomeres.html.

2. Jean-Pierre Burri. "Big Bang Philosophy." http://www.bigbang.org/.

3. Philip Gibbs and Jim Carr. "What is relativistic mass?." http://math.ucr.edu/home/baez/physics/Relativity/SR/mass.ht

4. The Ozone Hole Inc. "Solar Power." http://www.solcomhouse.com/solarpower.htm.

5. Backbone Consultants. "HyperFlight Primer On Quantum Mechanics". http://www.hyperflight.com/primer.htm.

6. Roto Grip. "STRIKE CELL™, Bowling Ball." http://www.rotogrip.com/products/balls/ball.asp?ballid=77.

7. National Geographic. "Virgin Birth Expected at Christmas By Komodo Dragon". http://news.nationalgeographic.com/news/2006/12/061220-virgin-dragons.html.

8. Aish.com Your life. Your Judaism. "Why Jews Don't Believe in Jesus". http://www.aish.com/jw/s/48892792.html.

9. Martin K. Barrack. "Personal Qualifications of the Messiah". http://www.secondexodus.com/html/jewishcatholicdialogue/personalqualifications.htm.

10. "The Belgian priest who invented the Big Bang theory shows up the modern canard about faith and science | CatholicHerald. co.uk." *CatholicHerald.co.uk | Breaking news and opinion from the online edition of Britainâ€™s leading Catholic newspaper.* N.p., n.d. Web. 13 Sept. 2013. <http://www.catholicherald. co.uk/commentandblogs/2012/10/03/the-belgian-priest-who-invented-the-big-bang-theory-shows-up-the-canard-about-faith-and-science/>.

11. "Home | The University of Tennessee, Knoxville | Department of Physics and Astronomy." *Home | The University of Tennessee, Knoxville | Department of Physics and Astronomy.* http://csep10. phys.utk.edu/astr162/lect/cosmology/forces.html, n.d. Web. 13 Sept. 2013. <http://www.phys.utk.edu>.

12. "Humans Broke Off Neanderthal Sex After Discovering Eurasia | LiveScience." *Science News â€ "Science Articles and Current Events | LiveScience.* N.p., n.d. Web. 13 Sept. 2013. <http://www.livescience.com/23730-neanderthals-modern-humans-interbreeding.html>.

13. "1 Kings 11—Solomon's Decline and Death." *Enduring Word Media.* N.p., n.d. Web. 13 Sept. 2013. <http://www. enduringword.com/commentaries/1111.htm>.

14. "Big Bang Theory." *Science—AllAboutScience.org.* N.p., n.d. Web. 13 Sept. 2013. <http://www.allaboutscience.org/big-bang-theory.htm>.

15. "Covenant of Works, Part 2 | Reformed Bible Studies & Devotionals at Ligonier.org." *Reformed Theology from R.C. Sproul: Ligonier Ministries.* N.p., n.d. Web. 13 Sept. 2013. <http://www. ligonier.org/learn/devotionals/covenant-works-part/>.

16. Ellis, Blake. "Transgender job seekers face uphill battle— Feb. 22, 2013." *CNNMoney—Business, financial and personal finance news.* N.p., n.d. Web. 13 Sept. 2013. <http://money.cnn. com/2013/02/22/pf/transgender-unemployment/index.html>.

17. "Fox News—Breaking News Updates | Latest News Headlines | Photos & News Videos." *Fox News—Breaking News Updates*

| *Latest News Headlines* | *Photos & News Videos.* (http://www. foxnews.com/story/0,2933,196642,00.html), n.d. Web. 13 Sept. 2013. <http://www.foxnews.com>.

18. "Gold, Bondi, and Hoyle | Everyday Cosmology." *Everyday Cosmology | connecting cosmology to real life.* N.p., n.d. Web. 13 Sept. 2013. <http://cosmology.carnegiescience.edu/timeline/1949/gold-bondi-hoyle>.

19. "HowMany.org—Population growth and the Environment | How overpopulation affects the U.S. and the World." *HowMany.org—Population growth and the Environment | How overpopulation affects the U.S. and the World.* N.p., n.d. Web. 13 Sept. 2013. <http://www.howmany.org>.

20. "NASA." *NASA.* http://spaceplace.nasa.gov/review/dr-marc-space/center-of-universe.html, n.d. Web. 13 Sept. 2013. <http://www.nasa.gov>.

21. "National Geographic—Inspiring People to Care About the Planet Since 1888." *National Geographic—Inspiring People to Care About the Planet Since 1888.* http://ngm.nationalgeographic. com/2008/03/god-particle/achenbach-text, n.d. Web. 13 Sept. 2013. <http://www.nationalgeographic.com>.

22. "National Geographic—Inspiring People to Care About the Planet Since 1888." *National Geographic—Inspiring People to Care About the Planet Since 1888.* http://news. nationalgeographic.com/news/2012/01/120106-virgin-birth-shark-dubai-science/, n.d. Web. 13 Sept. 2013. <http://www. nationalgeographic.com>.

23. "PBS: Public Broadcasting Service." *PBS: Public Broadcasting Service.* www.pbs.org/wgbh/nova/evolution/where-did-we-come-from.html, n.d. Web. 13 Sept. 2013. <http://www.pbs. org>.

24. "PBS: Public Broadcasting Service." *PBS: Public Broadcasting Service.* http://www.pbs.org/wgbh/nova/evolution/where-did-we-come-from.html, n.d. Web. 13 Sept. 2013. <http://www. pbs.org>.

25. "What is the "Second Death"?." *The Good News About God—Telling the Truth and Exposing Lies.* N.p., n.d. Web. 13 Sept. 2013. <http://www.goodnewsaboutgod.com/studies/seconddeath2.htm>.

26. "When did Satan fall from Heaven? | Creation Today." *Creation Today—Creation Science, Apologetics, Evangelism.* N.p., n.d. Web. 13 Sept. 2013. <http://www.creationtoday.org/when-did-satan-fall-from-heaven/>.

27. "http://www.sweetpoison.com/aspartame-information.html." *http://www.sweetpoison.com/aspartame-side-effects.html.* http://www.sweetpoison.com/about-janet-hull.html, n.d. Web. 12 Sept. 2013. < http://www.sweetpoison.com/about-janet-hull.html>.

28. "steady." *PBS: Public Broadcasting Service.* N.p., n.d. Web. 13 Sept. 2013. <http://www.pbs.org/wnet/hawking/universes/html/univ_steady.html>.

29. Michael Patton. "What Happened to the Twelve Apostles?." http://www.reclaimingthemind.org/blog/2007/09/what—happened-to-the-twelve-apostles/.

30. Fox News Network. "The Ethical Dilemmas of Immortality." http://www.foxnews.com/story/0,2933,196642,00.html.

31. Harvard Science Review. "It's The End of the World." http://www.hcs.harvard.edu/~hsr/pdfsspring2007/goyalcenterlayout.pdf.

32. The Bible Gateway. "King James Version." http://bibleresources.bible.com/bible_kjv.php.

33. David Steineker. "Ethanol Distillation System." www.InventHelp.com.

Study Guide

Written By: Lee Howell Steineker

How the study guide will help the reader? It is my hope the reader will take a more in depth look at the Chapters presented by going through the study guide and gain a more deeper understanding "to grasp how wide and long and high and deep is the love of Christ, and to know this love that surpasses knowledge—that you may be filled to the measure of all the fullness of God." (Ephesians 3:18) Further, it is my hope the reader will be more motivated to live out "The Greatest Commandment" in the adventures of life.

My testimony as a Christian:

I was raised by two wonderful parents and grew up going to Church. During my high school and college years I drifted away from a loving relationship with God. In my late 20's I reconnected to a Church family and began studying the Bible. Around that same time I experienced some trials and tribulations, such as the loss of my job and an auto-immune disease that caused my health to suffer. God continued to teach me perseverance, to be faithful, and blessed me abundantly with a wife, children, new job, as well as a great Church family. Praise God for friends, like my brother who continue to journey with me on learning to "grow in the grace and knowledge of our Lord and Savior, Jesus Christ." (2 Peter 3:18) I would like to encourage you to remain faithful during whatever season of life you are in, to walk daily with the Lord and seek His will. Jesus loves you.

Chapter 1   Introduction

The Bible says God is love (1 John 4:7-21) and the two greatest commandments (Matthew 22:37) instruct us to love God and love others. Is it easier for you to love God than love others? How does fear prevent us from loving God or others more effectively like the fear of what other people think? When we focus on the love God has for us and others, is it easier to want to love other people through prayer and action?

Why is it hard at times to follow God's will instead of our will?

Chapter 1 states: "A miracle is a record that an unprovable opposite has occurred."

Do you believe in miracles? Is it possible to believe in miracles and not God?

Reading, knowing and living God's truth equips Christians to sacrifice and have an eternal perspective. Make a list of who you look forward to being with in Heaven.

Where in your life have you disobeyed God in the sense of "eating from the Tree of knowledge of good and evil"? How is desiring to be like God or believing we can live without God, a dangerous path of self-suffiency instead of God dependency?

Like with Adam and Eve, there are consequences of our sins. The slippery slope often starts with one bite. Has God's gift of grace allowed more time for you to be in a right relationship with Him and others?

God desires for us to be holy, follow after Him and enjoy the blessings or even hardships (James 1:2-4) of this life. Where are you tempted to follow Satan and how best may you battle against temptation such as using the full armor of God in Ephesians 6:10-17?

Chapter 1 says "Eve wanted more". How is it possible to become content with less verses "wanting more". In the book, "The Lion, the Witch and the Wardrobe", The White Witch of Narnia offers Edmund Turkish Delight, which he eats and becomes consumed with wanting more instead of being content and desiring God more. Where has wanting more and more got you into trouble?

Pride, a hardened heart or a false religion can keep us from becoming a new creation in Christ. What does it mean to accept Christ, pick up your cross daily and be a new creation in Christ?

There is a danger in our lives that allows something to be in place of or above God and that is called an idol. Choices like an addition to sex can put our selfish desires above what God desires. God desires us to enjoy sex between a married man and woman but not when sex is the focus instead of pleasing God and one another. What would you say are the idols you face in your life?

Jesus said "the truth can set you free" (John 8:36). When in your life has being set free drawn you closer to a loving relationship with God?

Jesus spoke of the parable of the farmer and the seed in Matthew 13:18-23. Think of the people around you, such as family, neighbors, and co-workers. Where do you see the people God has placed in your path as fitting into the different places the seed fell?

A) rocky soil—love of God in their mind only

B) thorns—love of God in their soul and mind

C) good soil—love of God in their mind, soul and heart.

Please pray about what God can lead you to do to help "prepare the way" for others in your life to have a relationship with Jesus Christ.

Chapter 2   Total Existence Theory

The question posed at the beginning of the chapter concerns whether the universe is either finite or infinite. Our knowledge is finite whereas God is omnipotent. Is your love for God finite or infinite? For example, is your love ever conditional based on how you were raised and now how others treat you?

Is it easy or hard for you to love others unconditionally? Since love is a verb and requires action, how can you be more intentional in your love for God and others? Try to do one thing each day this week to demonstrate your love for God and others.

Theories like the Big Bang Theory or Steady State are theories that help show how man has a thirst for understanding and meaning in life. God has made earth and everything around it as a way to allow for exploration and discovery. When in your live have you had an "epiphany" of who God is and what He has done for you?

God took the time in Genesis 1:27 to make us in His image and make man from the dust of the ground as described in Genesis 2:7. Does the God particle help with understanding God's purpose with creating man and woman or the environment around us?

The delicate balance of the universe is amazing and there is plenty of evidence of Intelligent Design. Read Ephesians 3 verses 14-20 and ponder God's love.

Do you agree evil exists because of "free will"?

What can be done in the public education system to present a more balanced approach than just the Finite Universe resulting from the Big Bang? What can be gained by teaching the Bible and Creationism?

Chapter 3   Chemistry

Do you agree with the statement "love at first sight" or "good looking protons"? Have you ever began or ended a relationship because of good or bad chemistry?

The goal of Chapter three is to help us be better communicators and friends with other groups of people that they would not normally be friends. Is it easy for you to make new friends? Is there a neighbor or someone at work that you could start a friendship with or deepen a friendship?

How God designed each of us male and female as well as the chemistry of metallic bonding have an interesting impact on how well we form friendships. Take a minute to examine your friendships and think about the types of your close friendships.

Some of us are wired to be like Group 2 men that have excellent balance and a desire to be married and stay married where others may be like Paul in the Bible who was single and served others in other ways. No matter what ever point in life you are at right now, do your best to allow God's love to shine through you.

Do you have a friend that could be forgiven or is there a friend you have harmed that could be restored by asking forgiveness?

What do you consider harmful to relationships, such as divorce or an affair? What role does chemistry play in understanding our temptations and how to avoid them?

If you are married how do you decide who does what tasks? When is it healthy to trade or share tasks?

Do you agree with the statement in Chapter 3: "in a relationship the female is the one that typically holds on to the words exchanged."?

Chapter 4   White Light

In Genesis 1:3 "God said, let there be light, and there was light." In what areas of your life is God shedding light on your understanding of Him and your purpose in life?

Have you "seen the light" and confessed Jesus Lord of your life? It is as easy as ABC. First "accept" that God exists and desires a loving relationship with you. Next, "believe" that Jesus died on the cross for your sins. Finally, "confess" Jesus Lord of your life.

White Light possesses an array of colors and likewise there is an array of different kinds of people with different types of love languages. Fill in this blank with a person who is different than you and how you could love this type of person better _____.

A rainbow is caused by sunshine (white light) on water droplets that are in the air just after a rain shower. In the Bible the rainbow symbolizes a sign that God would not flood the earth again. Is there an area of your life that you could change to be more loving like a beautiful rainbow?

Albert Einstein changed our view of the universe and the physics. Find someone from history that has made significant discoveries or positive impact on our world and find out what role their faith did or did not have in shaping the person they became.

What did you find helpful in the authors presentation on light?

Chapter 5   Human Origin Theory

At this point in your life, why do you believe what you believe about Human Origin? How have family, friends or educators influenced what you believe about Human Origin?

How has God helped you understand more about Him through reading Genesis 1:1-3:17? What amazes you about God's creative ability? What are your thoughts about the fallen arch angel? God loves you, laid out His plan for us in Genesis and has a purpose for you now.

What does it mean to view one as a child of God?

Whether it's Charles Darwin's attempt to explain how humans came into being or your own attempt to follow a "Family Tree" to see where your family came from, the desire for history is told in His Story the Bible and continues today. What are you doing now in your current family that is going to have an eternal impact for the Kingdom of Heaven or even future generations?

Believing the virgin birth of Jesus Christ starts at Genesis 1:1. If you can believe that God can create the heavens and earth and man from the dust of the earth, is it possible that God could have created Jesus Christ from a virgin birth?

Chapter 6   Queen of the South

When does life begin? Is it at inception?

Why do you think the Queen of Sheba sought to test Solomon with hard questions?

Many times in the Bible, such as Job, people wrestled with God for answers to life's tough questions.

Have you ever "climbed the ladder of success" seeking more only to find you found less?

What was the goal of the Church stated in Chapter 6? How as a believer and follower of Jesus Christ my we as the body of Christ live out that goal? How can the Church be more effective in educating society on value of life in pregnant women?

Two consequences for women who choose to have an abortion were suggested in Chapter 6. How does your view of how someone takes a life or when someone takes a life, determine what their consequence should be? What should happen to the man who supports a woman who has an abortion?

Chapter 7   Matthew 22:37

Love is a decision, not an emotion. First we need to receive God's love then we may give God's love. What are some of the main reasons people choose not to receive God's love?

John 3:16 says, "For God so loved the world that he gave his one and only Son, that whoever believes in him shall not perish but have eternal life." Of the people you know, who do think will not be in Heaven and how could you pray for that person or at some point talk with them about the Kingdom of Heaven?

What unique talents has God blessed you with?

In the Bible, Jesus spoke in parables to describe the Kingdom of Heaven. Read through a few of the parables Jesus said and ask God shed more light and what those parables mean.

Do you ever find it easy or difficult to love the Lord in each of the three areas of 1) heart 2) mind 3) soul?

Acts 16:31 says, "Believe in the Lord Jesus, and you will be saved—you and your household." When your faith is tested by events in life like the loss of a family member that are trying or get you down, how can scriptures like Acts 16:31 help you to remember an eternal perspective?

Chapter 8   John the Baptist

When you read the name "John the Baptist" what comes to mind? What do remember most about him? What does it mean to "prepare the way" as John the Baptist and Jesus did? What are some ways you could help "prepare the way" for those around you who do not know Jesus or the two greatest commandments?

Why do you think some people believe that after they are baptized it does not matter so much what sins are done afterward? What negative impact happens from the "free ticket" mentality?

How would you describe the freeing power of repenting of your sins and asking God for the forgiveness of the wrong you have done to God and others in your life? Please take a moment now and ask God to forgive any sin in your life and what steps you could take to sin less.

Where do you see Satan trying to attack you or your family? There is no question the family continues to be under attack. Satan desires to break up the family or prevent families from being Christ centered. What have you done to strengthen your faith as a pre-emptive strike and counter-attack Satan's attempts?

Heaven or Hell, good verses evil are part of the choices free will allows. Free will is a great example of God's love for us. God desires us to be able to choose what we believe. There are places in this world where freedom is limited and preaching or teaching from the Bible is not allowed. If you could go on a missionary journey anywhere in the world where would you go?

Hate the sin not the sinner. In what ways is it possible for you to understand God more through how He reconciled us through Christ dying on the cross from the punishment of death? What happens when you reconcile with someone who harmed you or vice-versa?

Chapter 9   The Lord's Prayer

Have you ever thought about how valuable the sun is to sustaining life here on earth? Have you ever thought about how valuable the son (Jesus) is to not only sustaining an abundant life here on earth but providing a way to heaven?

What does it mean to do the will of God? What is the will of God in your life?

After reading Chapter 9, please consider reading and meditating on the Lord's Prayer in Matthew 6:9-13. How does it make you feel?

The Lord's Prayer is a wonderful example of how we may pray to Father God. Think about how Jesus prayed, when Jesus prayed, where Jesus prayed, why Jesus prayed or to whom Jesus prayed.

Giving and being generous is one way we may life out our faith and give thanks to God our father. What lessons have you been taught on giving and what do you experience when you give?

Chapter 10   God will Provide

God will provide. When you read the previous sentence, what is your first response? Is it God providing financially? Is it God providing an answer to a question? Is it God providing something like patience?

How hard is it to wait on God to provide? How much does God's provision and our participation play a role in the level of what is provided?

1 Corinthians 10:13 says, "No temptation has seized you except what is common to man. And God is faithful; he will not let you be tempted beyond what you can bear. But when you are tempted, he will also provide a way out so that you can stand up under it." What sin like revenge is tempting you with and pray about what way out God will provide?

Try to remember a time in your life when something was provided unexpectedly.

Jesus said, "It is more blessed to give than receive" (Acts 20:35). What inspires you to give?

What do you like or dislike about the proposed "medical bill estimate" website idea in Chapter 10?

Is there a risk that you have being considering to take but have not so far? What is that first step like Peter took to get out of the boat that you could take?

Chapter 11   The Chain of Command

When have you been inspired by a leader to dream, learn more, do more and become more as the John Quincy Adams quote states on the first page of Chapter 11? How did that leader inspire you?

How did Jesus lead others? What do you think was Jesus leadership style? Did Jesus lead based on who he was talking with?

Chain of commands varies based on the situation or organization. Do you look first to God for His desire on how you should live your life? Do you have an easy or hard time giving or following orders?

Deciding who to ask for help is an example where to go in a chain of command. Please take some time to examine the chain of commands in your life and evaluate if things are going well or if any changes could be made to improve communication.

There is God's general will for your life, like following His two greatest commandments and there is God's specific will for your life, like should I change jobs or not. How can trying to live like a Pharisee and changing jobs for the wrong reasons cause more problems than less problems in the end?

Sometimes God spoke directly to people in the Bible. Sometimes God used angels to speak to people. God even used a donkey to speak to Balaam. What can we learn from how God speaks to His children? What can we learn from how Paul tried to speak the truth in love on his travels?

Chapter 12   Child of God

Our identity, which defines who we are, is often based on how we are raised or it could even be what entertainment preoccupies us. What do you most identify with? How does having an eternal spirit as a child of God, provide more purpose in life here now and life in Heaven later?

Father, Son and Holy Spirit are described as the Trinity. Galatians 5:16 says, "So I say, live by the Spirit, and you will not gratify the desires of the sinful nature." Where is the Holy Spirit guiding you to desire loving God and others more than the sinful nature?

Please read Luke 10:25-37. What do we learn from these verses that teaches us about a vertical loving relationship with God and a horizontal loving relationship with others? Pray over understanding what it means to love God. What part does your soul play in loving God?

Have you ever tried memorizing scripture? One of the most quoted scriptures is John 3:16. Try to memorize John 3:16 and think about how much God loves you.

Go through the Bible and examine the life of Solomon and see where he "chased the wind" and came to the conclusion in Ecclesiastes 12:13-14. Talk with a grandparent, elderly neighbor or someone in a nursing home and ask what wisdom they have learned and what matters in the end.

Chapter 13   The Unforgivable Sin

Have you ever committed a sin in your life and felt it was "unforgiveable"? How could you ask God for help with sin in your life and repent (turn from) what draws you away from God? Read through Psalms and look for examples of "cries for help".

Knowing that Christ defeated Satan at the cross and Satan will receive his final judgment provides victory in Jesus. Should we be thankful and celebrate the victory? How does our culture today celebrate victories, such in sports and how could we be more focused on victory in Jesus?

When can beauty be a curse or give an advantage? How much is beauty in the eye of the beholder? Always remember what 1 Samuel chapter 16 verse 7 "But the Lord said to Samuel, "Do not consider his appearance or his height, for I have rejected him. The Lord does not look at the things man looks at. Man looks at the outward appearance, but the Lord looks at the heart." Read Mark 3:29.

When you think of what Jesus looked like, what picture comes to mind? Does Jesus look meek praying toward Heaven? Does Jesus look more masculine? Jesus was perfect and had all of the seven spiritual gifts listed in Romans 12. God has given you a spiritual gift and God wants you through the power of the Holy Spirit to use your gift and other talents to glorify God, love others, help prepare yourself for life after earth and help prepare the way for others for the arrival in the most indescribable Paradise of all...the Kingdom of Heaven.

Printed in the United States
By Bookmasters